"Clearly, this is the definitive guide to 529 Plans. It is a must read for anyone that needs a detailed understanding of the most important financial vehicle since the advent of the 401(k)."
—William L. Koleszar, *Chief Strategy Officer, BabyMint™, Inc.*

"An indispensable guide to understanding one of the most significant savings, tax and estate planning tools to come around in years."
—Eric Kobren, *"Fidelity Insight"*

"Richard Feigenbaum and David Morton offer a user-friendly guide to this powerful new financial instrument—complete with practical examples of how they apply in real-life situations. They have produced an important addition to college admissions literature."
—Edward B. Fiske, author of *The Fiske Guide to Colleges*

"A great, new guide to understanding 529s."
—*Alliance Capital*

"An outstanding guide to 529 Plans...the best, new way for families to save for college."
—Jim Fadule, *President, Upromise™ Investments*

THE
529
COLLEGE
SAVINGS PLAN

RICHARD A. FEIGENBAUM
ATTORNEY AT LAW
AND
DAVID J. MORTON
MANAGING DIRECTOR OF INVESTMENTS

SPHINX® PUBLISHING
AN IMPRINT OF SOURCEBOOKS, INC.®
NAPERVILLE, ILLINOIS
www.SphinxLegal.com

First Edition, 2002

Published by: **Sphinx® Publishing, An Imprint of Sourcebooks, Inc.®**

Naperville Office
P.O. Box 4410
Naperville, Illinois 60567-4410
630-961-3900
Fax: 630-961-2168
www.sourcebooks.com
www.SphinxLegal.com

This publication is designed to provide accurate and authoritative information in regard to the subject matter covered. It is sold with the understanding that the publisher is not engaged in rendering legal, accounting, or other professional service. If legal advice or other expert assistance is required, the services of a competent professional person should be sought. *From a Declaration of Principles Jointly Adopted by a Committee of the American Bar Association and a Committee of Publishers and Associations*

The information in this book is for educational purposes only. It is not intended as specific investment advice. Investors should consult a tax advisor or investment advisor to determine state tax consequences and suitability requirements of any investment.

This product is not a substitute for legal advice.

Disclaimer required by Texas statutes.

Library of Congress Cataloging-in-Publication Data
Feigenbaum, Richard A.
    The 529 College Savings Plan / Richard A. Feigenbaum and David J. Morton.-- 1st ed.
        p. cm.
    Includes index.
    ISBN 1-57248-238-9 (alk. paper)
    1. College costs--United States. 2. Savings accounts--United States. 3. Finance,
Personal--United States. I. Title: Five-twenty-nine College Savings Plan. II. Morton,
David J., 1969- III. Title.

LB2342 .F42 2002
378.3'8--dc21
                                                                    2002075792

Printed and bound in the United States of America.
VHG Paperback — 10 9 8 7 6 5 4 3 2 1

ACKNOWLEDGMENT

We are grateful for the assistance and expert analysis provided us by Rachel Seraphin in connection with her review of the many different state plans and to Courtney Cyr for her efforts in connection with editing and chapter summaries. We are also grateful to Michael Capobianco for his expertise, encouragement and ability to help us keep our focus.

DEDICATION

We dedicate this book to our children: Alexandra, Michael, Oliver and Brenner, who inspire us and remind us each day why our goal, and the goal of many families, is to provide our children the best education possible now and in the future.

A debt of gratitude is owed to our spouses, Eleanor and Delphine, for their patience and support of our work and this project.

TABLE OF CONTENTS

INTRODUCTION xiii

FREQUENTLY ASKED QUESTIONS xv

CHAPTER 1: THE BASICS OF 529 PLANS 1

    Internal Revenue Code Section 529

    What the College Savings Account Really Is

    Establishing a College Savings Account

    Rules, Rules, Rules

    Future Changes in the Law

    Chapter 1—At a Glance

CHAPTER 2: HELPING TO SAVE FOR COLLEGE 15

    Taxes and Tax Deferred Savings

    College Savings Accounts Versus other
        Methods of Saving for College

    College Savings Plan/Section 529 Advantage

    Coordination of Hope Scholarship Credit with
        Section 529 College Savings Plans

    Chapter 2—At a Glance

CHAPTER 3: TAXATION OF COLLEGE SAVINGS PLANS 33

    Basic Tax Rules

    Qualified Higher Education Expenses

    Eligible Institution

    Taxes on Distributions

    Deductions for Contributions—Federal

    Deductions for Contributions—State

State Taxation on Withdrawals from a
   College Savings Plan
Chapter 3—At a Glance

CHAPTER 4: BENEFICIARY PLANNING 45
The Basics
Changing the Beneficiary
Making Changes to an Existing College Savings Plan
Chapter 4—At a Glance

CHAPTER 5: OWNERSHIP OF A 529 PLAN 53
Lifetime Issues
Transfer at Death
Trusts as Owners
Chapter 5—At a Glance

CHAPTER 6: THE ROLE OF THE ADVISOR 57
Issues for the Advisor
Role of the Advisor in Corporate-Sponsored Plans
Chapter 6—At a Glance

CHAPTER 7: ESTATE PLANNING AND
   THE COLLEGE SAVINGS PLAN 63
Federal Estate Planning Basics
College Savings Plans—Estate Planning Rules
Creative Estate Planning
The "Double Dip" Opportunity
The Unintended Gift Tax Consequence
Ownership Issues and Estate Planning
Post Death Trust Issues
Death of a College Savings Plan Beneficiary
Strange Possibilities
Chapter 7—At a Glance

CHAPTER 8: THE "NEW" EMPLOYEE BENEFIT 75
    Understanding Employee Benefit Plans
    Expanding Benefit Plans
    Adding 529 Plans to the Package
    Determining if Your Employer Offers a 529 Plan
    A Word of Caution
    Chapter 8—At a Glance

CHAPTER 9: SCHOLARSHIP PROGRAMS AND THE 529 PLAN 83
    Traditional Charities and College Savings Plans
    Establishing the Scholarship Program
    Universities and Colleges—Compensation Planning
    Corporate-Sponsored College Savings Accounts—
        Compensation Planning
    Chapter 9—At a Glance

CHAPTER 10: THE FUTURE OF 529 PLANS 93
    Upromise™ and BabyMint™
    Affinity Programs
    Chapter 10—At a Glance

GLOSSARY 97

APPENDIX A: INTERNAL REVENUE CODE SECTION 529 105

APPENDIX B: STATE BY STATE SUMMARY OF
        PLANS AND PLAN MANAGERS 111

APPENDIX C: STATE PROGRAM INTERNET LINKS 215

INDEX 221

INTRODUCTION

In an era of ever increasing taxation promoted to the public under the guise of "tax simplification," Congress has taken the single greatest step ever towards solving the college savings dilemma. Year after year families have struggled to save sufficient funds to provide a quality college education for their children. In the face of this struggle college costs have steadily increased and the earnings on the money families have saved has been taxed heavily. As families responded by shifting savings and investments to their children's names to minimize the income tax, Congress countered with a set of rules (known as the "kiddie tax") specifically designed to continue taxing these accounts.

Then...in 1996 Congress had a change of heart. In a quiet, lightning type strike, the world of saving for college was turned on its head. With the passing of a new law and the creation of a new Internal Revenue Code (IRC) section, Congress changed the landscape of saving for college forever. On August 20, 1996 Code Section 529 became law, and now families have for the first time a tax advantaged way to save for college and related expenses. Section 529, and these "529 plans" as they have become known, allow for the investment of money on a tax-free basis if the invested funds are used for a "qualified higher education expense" (IRC, Section (Sec.) 529 (c)). For the first time, money can be invested for growth without any taxation and can be withdrawn tax free if used for college and related expenses.

As with many laws, its true impact can be understood only over time. Even at this early point in its life, Section 529 has generated a myriad of planning opportunities never before considered. In addition to using the Section 529 Plan for saving money for college, these 529 Plans allow a family to transfer money from one generation to the next, free of any income, estate, or gift taxes as long as the money is invested for "qualified higher education expenses." In addition, these

College Savings Plans allow colleges and universities the ability to provide a tax-free benefit in the form of tuition assistance to children of college employees. These plans can be provided in a favorable way that will avoid including some of these benefits in the employee's income for income tax purposes. It is clear then that these Section 529 College Savings Plans have changed forever our most basic understanding of how gifts can be made to children and grandchildren.

Our goal in creating this working manual is to explore each of the opportunities afforded by these 529 plans, analyze in-depth the positive and the negative, open the eyes of the consumer and the professional planners to the endless bounds of creative planning that now exists, and to caution where necessary against spur of the moment decisions in tapping into this new opportunity.

Given the emerging nature of this field, and the complexity of the tax and investment issues it raises, this book is only intended to provide general information on the subject of College Savings Plans. Please consult with a qualified advisor to discuss your personal investment issues, and the appropriateness of utilizing a College Savings Plan as part of your overall financial planning strategy.

FREQUENTLY ASKED QUESTIONS

1. What is a 529 College Savings Plan?

A 529 College Savings Plan is a savings plan established and maintained by a state to assist families in saving for college. These plans are created under federal law and allow for tax deferred growth on the investments and tax free withdrawal from the account if the assets are used for "qualified higher education expenses." (see Chapter 1.)

2. How do I open a College Savings Plan account?

Each state has a plan either in place or under development and the plan can be accessed via the internet or by contacting the financial services firm retained by the state to administer their plan. See the Appendix to obtain websites, addresses, phone numbers and web links. (see Chapter 1.)

3. What are the benefits of a College Savings Plan?

The College Savings Plan allows assets to appreciate tax deferred and provide tax free withdrawals if the assets are used for qualified higher education expenses. (see Chapter 1.)

4. Are there income limits or thresholds that phase out or eliminate the ability to contribute to a College Savings Plan account?

No. There are no income or other limits on the ability to contribute to an account other than the maximum funding level each state designates for its particular plan. (see Chapter 1.)

5. Who can establish a College Savings Plan?

Any person can create a College Savings Plan for any other person or for the benefit of themselves. As long as the assets are withdrawn for use for qualified higher education expenses the growth on the investments will be tax free. This creates an opportunity where people can begin saving for possible graduate school or professional school later on in life and not only for children's higher education expenses. (see Chapter 2.)

6. Once the College Savings account is opened and the beneficiary is named, can we change the beneficiary?

The College Savings account allows for the change of beneficiary at any time by the account owner. Certain beneficiary changes are tax free and other changes result in taxation. Care must be had in making beneficiary changes. (see Chapter 4.)

7. Can the owner of a College Savings Plan account close the account and take back all of the money?

Yes. The owner of a College Savings Plan account can withdraw all the funds in an account at any time. This will lead to income taxation on the earnings on the account as well as a 10% penalty for withdrawing the funds and not using them for qualified higher education expenses. (see Chapter 5.)

8. Who is allowed to be a beneficiary?

Any person can be a beneficiary whether it is a related person such as a child, grandchild, spouse, etc., or someone who is not related. The beneficiary must be a US citizen or a resident alien. You can also establish the account for yourself as the beneficiary. (see Chapter 4.)

9. Once an account is established, who retains control over the investment decisions?

Each Plan Manager develops a number of model portfolios for which you can choose to invest your savings in. Federal law requires that the consumer have no control over investment choices, and as such, Plan Managers have provided a large number of options for the consumer to select from. (see Chapter 5.)

10. Can anyone contribute to a 529 account maintained for a beneficiary?

Each state's plan is slightly different, however, as a general rule most Advisor type plans allow for any person to make contributions into an existing 529 account. (see Chapter 2.)

11. What are the most common investment options given by Plan Managers?

The most common investment offerings include age based allocation investments which are geared towards your child's age and the year in which he or she will attend college. There are also asset allocation investments, growth investments, aggressive and conservative investments as well as a variety of equity and fixed income options within most plans. (see Chapter 6.)

12. Can you change investment options once they have been selected for the College Savings account?

The investment option chosen for a College Savings Plan account can only be changed once each year. However, each time a new contribution is made to a College Savings Account, a different election can be made with respect to how these newly contributed assets are to be invested. (see Chapter 6.)

13. Is there a federal deduction for contributing to a College Savings Plan?

No. At the present time, there is no federal deduction for contributions to a College Savings Plan. (see Chapter 3.)

14. Are there state deductions for contributions to a College Savings Plan?

Yes. Many of the states have laws allowing for a deduction on personal income tax returns for contributions made to College Savings Plans. (see Chapter 3.)

15. Are the withdrawals from a College Savings Plan free from federal income tax?

A withdrawal from a College Savings Plan is free of federal income tax if the proceeds are used for qualified higher education expenses at an accredited institution. Generally, these schools are accredited if they participate in the Federal Student Aid Program. You can contact the Plan Manager for the state in which the school is located or contact the school directly to determine whether they meet this standard. (see Chapter 3.)

16. Are withdrawals for College Savings Plans free from state income tax?

Withdrawals from a College Savings Plan may be taxed to you depending on your state of residency. Many states have adopted the federal exclusion of these plan proceeds from income tax and as such these states will not tax distribution. Other states do not have their own income tax and again they would not be taxing distributions. Still other states have state income taxes and have not adopted federal law, in which case these states will tax distributions from a College Savings Plan account. (see Chapter 3.)

17. Can the College Savings Plan assets be used for all colleges and universities?

The College Savings Plan assets can be used for *most* accredited institutions of higher education in the United States. Generally, those schools, whether college or graduate school, vocational or trade school, that participate in the federal student aid program are eligible for participation in the College Savings Plan. (see Chapter 3.)

18. How do you change the beneficiary on a College Savings Plan account?

Each Plan Manager will maintain their own forms for purpose of updating beneficiaries on accounts so that a change of beneficiary form can be signed to reflect a new beneficiary. (see Chapter 4.)

19. Does the changing of a beneficiary generate an income tax?

The relationship of the new beneficiary to the old beneficiary may determine whether there is an income tax, penalty tax or gift tax on the change of beneficiary. (see Chapters 3 and 4.)

20. Can I borrow money from the plan or use the plan as security for a loan?

No. Federal law specifically provides that you cannot use the account as collateral for a loan or borrow money from the plan. (see Chapter 1.)

21. What happens if money is withdrawn from the plan and not used for "qualified higher education expenses"?

When assets are withdrawn from the plan and not used for "qualified higher education expenses," an income tax must be paid by the owner on the assets withdrawn, as well as a 10% penalty on the income. (see Chapter 3.)

22. Who will own my account if I pass away before the account is fully utilized?

Under the existing ownership rules, an account owner has the ability to name a successor owner on the account if he or she should die. If no successor owner is named, then the owner's Last Will and Testament will determine who the new owner will be. (see Chapter 5.)

23. How does the College Savings Plan affect qualification for financial aid?

Under existing rules, a College Savings Account will be treated as an asset of the owner and not an asset of the beneficiary. For this reason, care should be given to structuring ownership of the College Savings Account to be certain it minimizes its impact on obtaining financial aid. (see Chapter 4.)

24. What are Upromise™ and BabyMint™, and how do they relate to a College Savings Plan?

Upromise™, Inc. and BabyMint™, Inc. are membership programs that obtains "free" contributions from corporations with whom consumers do business. These corporations provide contributions to a College Savings Plan account to a participant who purchases their goods. (see Chapter 10.)

25. Are College Savings Accounts taxed to the owner if the owner should die?

The College Savings Plan Account is not taxed to the owner should the owner pass away while retaining control of the College Savings account unless the owner had made a large gift and was prorating the annual gift tax exclusion over a number of years and died during the term of years. (see Chapters 3 and 5.)

26. Can the College Savings Plan Account be obtained through an employer and be payroll deducted?

Yes. College Savings Plan accounts are becoming a popular voluntary corporate benefit and afford the employee the same College Savings Plan opportunity at a lower cost and allows for the use of payroll deduction. Much like the popularity of the 401(k) benefit, a College Savings Plan that is obtained through an employer is more likely to be used by the employee then if they had to secure such an account on their own. The College Savings Plan as a voluntary employee benefit enhances the likelihood that people will save on a periodic basis for college expenses. (see Chapter 8.)

27. What happens if the beneficiary of a College Savings Account chooses not to go to college?

A College Savings Plan allows for the owner of the account to change the beneficiary of the account at any time. To make this change is as simple as signing a change of beneficiary form with the Plan Manager. Depending on the blood relationship of the original beneficiary to the new beneficiary, the change of beneficiary may be a tax-free change. In some circumstances, if the new beneficiary is not "a member of the family" of the old beneficiary, then the owner may be subjected to income taxes and penalty tax. (See Chapter 4.)

28. Do I need to be a resident of the state in which the College Savings Plan is sponsored?

Each state has its own rules as to who can invest in the state's home plan. A review of Appendix B will highlight the many differences among the plans, including those which allow non-residents of the state to use their College Savings Plan. (see Appendix B.)

29. Does the College Savings Plan "sunset" at the end of 2010?

Yes. Under current federal tax law, the College Savings Plan is scheduled to "sunset" (come to an end) on December 31, 2010. By the very nature of the sunset law, Code Section 529 will cease to exist after that date and these College Savings Plans will no longer be given favorable tax benefits on earnings. This may result in these accounts being subjected to income tax and possibly the penalty tax. However, commentators have discussed this issue at length and generally concur that it is *unlikely* that the sunset provision will be left in place. (see Chapter 10.)

30. Can an employer establish a College Savings Plan as a benefit for its employees?

Yes. The use of a College Savings Plan as a voluntary employee benefit is becoming a popular employee retention tool. Much like 401Ks and other group provided benefits, the corporate provided 529 College Savings Plan can be obtained for the employees at a reduced fee. These corporate provided College Savings Plans are entirely portable and are not tied to employment with a particular company. (see Chapter 8.)

31. Can I establish a College Savings Plan for myself and/or my spouse?

Depending on the state's plan, you may be able to establish a College Savings Account for yourself or your spouse. If you or your spouse decide to go to college, those funds can be used for those education expenses. Another reason to do this is to begin saving for a child who has not yet been born, in an effort to begin the tax deferred savings afforded by these College Savings Plan. In addition, funding an account for yourself in anticipation of a grandchild as a wealth transfer tool may be a reasonable estate planning opportunity. (see Chapter 7.)

32. Can a person be a beneficiary of more than one College Savings Plan?

Yes. A person can be beneficiary of as many College Savings Plans as he or she likes. Each state's plan mandates a maximum funding level for that state's plan, however, there is no requirement that all of a particular beneficiary's plans be in one state (see Chapter 1.)

33. Can one beneficiary have College Savings Plans in more than one state and fund each plan to its maximum level?

Yes. Under existing law, there is no prohibition from funding as many College Savings Plans as you would like to the maximum level fro the beneficiary. However, this tactic is likely to raise scrutiny from the I.R.S. and may be treated as tax evasion—not an appropriate College Savings technique. (see Chapter 1.)

34. If the owner of a College Savings Account needs nursing home care, will the College Savings Account be lost to the nursing home expense?

The simple answer is that there is no clear answer yet. Once a gift is made into a College Savings Account the money in the account should no longer be available for the owners debts and expenses. Unfortunately, the issue of whether money in a College Savings Account can be lost to the owner's nursing home expenses is based on state law. Each state has their own rules as to what assets will be available for nursing home expenses.(see Appendix C.)

THE BASICS OF 529 PLANS

Few things can keep a parent awake at night like the seemingly ominous task of saving for a child's (or children's) college education. Thanks to recent action by Congress, saving for college has become a slightly easier task. Internal Revenue Code Section 529 has created the single greatest savings opportunity in many years.

INTERNAL REVENUE CODE SECTION 529

Internal Revenue Code Section 529 (to be consistent throughout this work, we will call the governing law "Section 529") is a newly created tax law that allows each state to create their own Prepaid Tuition Plan and/or a College Savings Plan. Congress designed these new plans to help people save money for future college expenses. The idea behind these plans is to be certain that money saved for college is not subjected to tax during the time it is saved or the accumulation stage. This way families can attempt to keep pace with college costs without the additional, ever increasing burden of taxes.

The *Prepaid Tuition Plan*, one of two new plans created by Code Section 529, is established by each state. It allows for the purchase of tuition credits (like class credits when attending college) for use at participating colleges typically within the state's borders. These credits are held until the child attends college and are then redeemed for the number of credits purchased. Regardless of how much more the tuition is at the time of redemption, if the credits are used at a participating educational institution, the credits purchased long ago are used as full payment of the current tuition.

For example:

In 2001, Mary opened a prepaid tuition account as established by her home state, New Hampshire, for the benefit of her son, Phillip, age 12. Mary purchased 8 semesters of credits (4 years) and paid the tuition expense of $40,000 ($5,000 per semester). In 2007, when Phillip begins attending college (one that is affiliated with the plan), the first semester's tuition expense is $8,000. When the funds are used to pay tuition, the credits originally purchased for $5,000 satisfies in full the total tuition cost of $8,000. No income is recognized by the IRS as income for tax purposes and so no one needs to include any income on his or her tax return for the $3,000.00 *appreciation* (difference) on the tuition credits.

Since the Prepaid Tuition Plan affords little flexibility and other planning opportunities, little will be mentioned in this book on these plans. Rather, the focus will be on the *College Savings Accounts* or *529 Accounts*, as they have become known. (They are also commonly referred to as *529 Plans*. All three names refer to the same concept.)

While the law creating these College Savings Accounts is simple in nature, the application is anything but simple for the consumer. There are many reasons for this, none as important as the state-by-state differences among the plans. The law creating 529 Accounts allows each state to develop its own version of the College Savings Account, creating limitations, tax benefits, funding limits, rules, and regulations as it may choose. As long as a particular state's program meets the basic Internal Revenue Service (IRS) criteria for being a 529 Plan, the consumer will not be subjected to any tax on the investment gains while the assets are growing. The consumer will be able to take money out tax-free if used for *qualified higher education expenses*, all as provided by Section 529. (See page 34 for an explanation of qualified higher education expenses.)

For example:
In 2001, Mary opened a College Savings Account as established by the State of Maryland (and administered by T. Rowe Price) for the benefit of her son, Steve, age 12. The initial deposit was $20,000. In 2007, when Steve begins attending college, there is a total of $35,000 in the College Savings Account. When the funds are used to pay tuition, a portion of each payment is made up of the income earned on the investment (the $15,000 appreciation). If the College Savings Account is used for tuition, room, board, etc., then no one needs to include any income on

their tax return. The $15,000 appreciation completely avoids all forms of taxation. ▉

WHAT THE COLLEGE SAVINGS ACCOUNT REALLY IS

The College Savings Account is an investment account managed by a financial service firm. At the time of this publication, there are more than 30 institutional providers of a College Savings Account (529 Plans) of one form or another. When the opportunity presented itself in late 1996 and early 1997 after Congress enacted Section 529, investment firms made a choice as to whether or not to participate in this state-by-state program. Firms presently participating include many of the investment and mutual fund companies widely recognized across the country, such as:

- Fidelity Investments;
- Putnam;
- T.Rowe Price;
- TIAA/CREF;
- Salomon Smith Barney;
- ManuLife;
- MFS;
- State Street;
- Merrill Lynch; and,
- Alliance Capital.

Throughout this book we will refer to these investment houses as the *Plan Manager*.

These Individual College Savings Accounts have been given different names by the different Plan Managers, such as:

- Unique College Investing Plan;
- NJ Best Plan;
- College Save;
- CollegeBound Fund;
- Tomorrow's Scholar; and,
- NextGen College Investing Plan.

Contact the appropriate Plan Manager for specific information concerning the plan, including risks and expenses.

It seems to make sense that an *institutional approach* (that is to remove the management of the investments from the individual to the professional) to these

---

▉ *The example is provided for informational purposes only and does not reflect the actual performance of any investment. All programs involve investment risk, including the loss of principle. State taxes may be applicable.*

investments will be more efficient than allowing each person to self-direct his or her investments (as in a 401(k) or IRA). Only time will tell if the institutional investor will be able to live up to this goal.

ESTABLISHING A COLLEGE SAVINGS ACCOUNT

Establishing a College Savings Account is as simple as completing an application with one of the Plan Managers. Completing the application and getting started is relatively simple. As will be explored in some detail, much like any financial investment, there are many different choices available for investing the assets. You must give thought to the time length, risk tolerance, and available investment options within the College Savings Account before you settle on an investment strategy.

NOTE: *Due to the complexity of investing in the College Savings Plan, we strongly suggest that you obtain advice from a qualified financial advisor.*

RULES, RULES, RULES

Anticipating that like any newly created *tax benefit* there would be those looking to live within the loopholes, the law is clear as to what is required of each state and of the consumer to achieve the benefits of tax-free growth on investments. To qualify for special tax treatment, federal tax law requires that the account must meet the following basic requirements:

- The account must be created under a state's 529 Plan.
- The account may only receive cash contributions; not stocks, securities or other business interests.
- No one—whether the owner, contributor or beneficiary of the account—can have investment control over the account. Only the state—or its delegated investment firm—may direct the investments.
- Only certain maximum levels of funding are allowed.
- The College Savings Account cannot be pledged as collateral or security.
- The program, as administered by the states, must provide a separate accounting for each beneficiary of a plan.
- The College Savings Account *must* be used for *qualified higher education expenses*.

• The College Savings Account funds *must* be used at an *eligible educational institution* to have all gains and appreciation be tax-free at the time of distribution.

✦ THE ACCOUNT MUST BE CREATED UNDER A STATE'S 529 PLAN

By requiring the different states to each adopt its own plan (rather than a uniform national plan), each state can tailor and modify the plan as it may see fit. This will allow for changes and improvements as the years go on.

While the industry is still in its infancy, differences among the states have started to occur and changes are being adopted on a frequent basis. Understanding the differences among these state plans, when coupled with both the many investment options and the returns on the account assets, can help a well-informed consumer select the appropriate College Savings Account. It can also confuse the consumer, who without a professional advisor, may wander aimlessly among the options. This may result in an inability to even get started opening an account.

Differences Among the Plans

Some College Savings Accounts are only available to those who reside in their own state (i.e. Kentucky, Louisiana and New Jersey). Some plans are available to non-residents, but only through a broker who typically will charge a sales commission or an annual fee during the period of time the assets are invested in the plan. (See Appendix B for additional state information.)

Each state has its own rules about whether a resident investing in his or her home state's plan gets a special tax deduction. In addition, each state has its own rules about whether the withdrawal of funds from an account will be tax-free or taxable at the time of withdrawal.

Some plans have enrollment fees, an annual account maintenance fee, asset-based management fees, and an underlying fund expense. These fees are often in addition to that which is paid to the advisor assisting in the opening of the College Savings Account.

There are also differences stemming from the choice of investment options, or lack of options. Some plans have investment choices based on the consumer's preference or tolerance for risk (i.e. growth, balanced, aggressive growth, bond fund) and exposure to the marketplace. To gain a competitive edge, the Plan Managers continue to increase the consumer's options in an effort to have you feel you have some measure of control over the selection of investments.

✦THE ACCOUNT MAY ONLY RECEIVE CASH CONTRIBUTIONS; NOT STOCKS, SECURITIES OR OTHER BUSINESS INTERESTS

Under the law creating College Savings Plans, it is absolutely clear that only cash can be used to open or contribute to a College Savings Plan. This seemingly innocent requirement does create an issue for those who have been saving for college for some time now. For many years the traditional approach to saving for college has been to utilize an account titled in the child's name under the Uniform Gift to Minor's Act (UGMA) or its more modern relative, the Uniform Transfers to Minor Act (UTMA).

Governed by individual state's laws, these UTMA/UGMA savings accounts are taxable investment accounts, with all taxable income taxed to the child owner. Under these "kiddie tax" laws, income and capital gains of a child under 14 are taxable to the parents, and after age 14, are taxable to the child. Certainly, those with existing accounts will seek a way to transfer the existing account into a College Savings Account.

Unfortunately, the UGMA/UTMA account is normally not invested in cash, and would require that all the investments in the account be sold and converted to cash before the money could be transferred to a College Savings Plan. This *liquidation* would result in taxable income if the account had *appreciated* (gone up) in value. As is explained in Chapter 3, there are other state law issues created when trying to transfer a UTMA/UGMA into a College Savings Plan in addition to this "sticky" tax issue.

✦NO ONE CAN HAVE INVESTMENT CONTROL OVER THE ACCOUNT

Only the state or its Plan Manager (the designated investment firm) may direct the investments. The owner, contributor or beneficiary of the account cannot. For the consumer, this means that there is a loss of control over the investing of assets. For many this may be the best possible thing. For others, it will create a frustration over seemingly lost opportunities.

NOTE: *The conference reports from Congress in 1998 indicate that this element of the plan was of great importance. For this reason, they amended the 529 law to add that no person may "directly or indirectly" direct the investment of any contributions to the plan or income earned.*

To provide more flexibility to the consumer without violating this mandate, the Plan Managers began offering more than just *age-based* investment options. Many Plan Managers now allow for *risk-adjusted* options within these age-based approaches. For instance, Putnam Investments, operating as Plan Manager for the Ohio Tuition Trust Authority, has different investment options available. The State of New Hampshire Plan, administered and maintained by Fidelity Investments, has eight different age-based investment choices as well as three *static* portfolios that are not age-based.

When a College Savings Account is opened, the person who opens the account is very often labeled the *owner*. The owner is the person who has the ability to name the *beneficiary*, change the beneficiary from time to time, and is the person who has the power to withdraw funds from the account. (See Chapters 4 and 5 on what a beneficiary is and the issues affecting him or her.) While being prohibited from having direct control over investments, the account owner can gain some measure of control by searching for a Plan Manager that provides the options that meet with the account owner's liking.

Given that the numerous Plan Managers will each have their own selection of funds and alternative investment options, account owners may look for opportunities to *chase* the best return in the marketplace. (Chase means to try to time the market by jumping in and out of investments.) To prevent an account owner from gaining control (indirectly) of the investments by shifting from one Plan Manager to another, the law prohibits the transfer of an account more than one time per year. The following should help:

> For example:
> In 2000, Maye opened a College Savings Plan as established by New Hampshire for the benefit of Sean, age 12. Maye invested in the Plan Manager's Age-Based 2008 Fund. After one-year she grew frustrated over the Fund's performance and decided to move the account to another Plan Manager administering a different state's College Savings

Account. In so doing, she selected a more aggressive investment option, which was more suited to her liking. The transfer to the new plan does not violate the rules and does not create any income tax consequence for Maye or Sean. She made only one transfer after one year. ■

For example:

In 2000, Mary opened a College Savings Plan as established by New Hampshire for the benefit of her son, Phillip, age 12. She invested in the Plan Manager's Age-Based 2008 Fund. After only six months, Mary grew frustrated over the Fund's performance and decided to move the account to another Plan Manager administering a different state's College Savings Account. In so doing, Mary selected a more aggressive investment option, which was more suited to her liking. The transfer to the new plan *does* violate the rules (she made a change before the 1 year period ended), and *does* create taxable income for Mary or Phillip. ■

✦ONLY CERTAIN MAXIMUM LEVELS OF FUNDING ARE ALLOWED

Remember, these plans are designed to be for the purpose of saving for college. Parents can save for children; grandparents for grandchildren; charities can save for scholarships; aunts, uncles—everyone can save for everyone—but not too much. Even as expensive as college is, there is a limit. The law only allows for the saving of money for *qualified higher education expenses*, and that is all. Since the law allows each state to implement based on its own sets of rules, this is one area that will vary from state to state. As you compare state by state plans, you can see differences in the maximum funding level.

For instance, in the state of Maine, the maximum funding level is $225,000, while in New Hampshire, the maximum is $233,240. Most states are close in total maximum funding being somewhere in the $225,000 range. In reviewing the participation handbooks for the various Plan Managers, you can determine the rationale for that particular state.

The way it is supposed to be done, as provided by regulations, is by determining the estimated cost of tuition, fees, and room and board of a student attending five years of undergraduate school at the most expensive school in the state. So you can see that on a state-by-state basis, this amount should not vary much. As of this date,

Arkansas has the lowest total funding limit, presently set at $175,000 per beneficiary of an account opened under the Arkansas College Savings Plan.

The value to fully funding a College Savings Account goes beyond the ability to adequately provide for a child's college education. As a wealth transfer tool, the fully-funded 529 Plan can create substantial estate tax, gift tax and generation-skipping transfer tax savings for families of wealth. As will be discussed in Chapter 7, a College Savings Plan has expanded our estate planning opportunities far beyond what was likely intended when Congress enacted this law.

✦ THE COLLEGE SAVINGS ACCOUNT CANNOT BE PLEDGED AS COLLATERAL OR SECURITY

As a society, we tend to borrow too much, too often. However, the law makes it clear that the 529 Account is not allowed to be used as *collateral* for a loan or other debt. You cannot pledge or borrow against the 529 Plan. This means that the money really will be used for college unless the money is withdrawn. In that case, there would be a *disqualifying distribution*.

By preventing the account owner from borrowing against or pledging the College Savings Account for his or her loans or debts, these assets will truly be "hands off" and the assets will grow for college expenses. This puts the consumer in a position of either finding other sources for short-term borrowing or completely withdrawing assets from the College Savings Plan and incurring both the income tax and a 10% penalty on the income withdrawn. Congress' intention was to make this disqualifying distribution a costly exercise to act as a deterrent from short term borrowing.

✦ THE PROGRAM MUST PROVIDE A SEPARATE ACCOUNTING FOR EACH BENEFICIARY OF A PLAN

It seems obvious, but the law makes it clear, nonetheless. A Plan Manager must provide a statement of each beneficiary's account, providing details (at least annually) as follows:

- contributions during the accounting period;
- account value;
- earnings; and,
- distributions.

Most Plan Managers send a quarterly account statement. The law provides that if the Plan Manager does not account at least annually, then they must make the information available upon your request.

✦THE COLLEGE SAVINGS ACCOUNT MUST BE USED FOR "QUALIFIED HIGHER EDUCATION EXPENSES"

To get the tax-free investment gains in the 529 plan at the time of distribution, it is clear that the funds must be for *qualified higher education expenses*. If some or all of the distribution is not used for these qualified expenses, then the owner of the account will have to report on his or her tax return the portion of the withdrawal that is a gain or profit. This gain or profit must then be placed on the account owner's tax return and taxed as ordinary income.

In addition, there is a 10% *penalty tax* on the income or gains earned. This penalty acts as a true deterrent for using these assets for anything other than qualified higher education expenses. The basic premise to the plan is that the money saved in this *tax-favored* savings account is intended to be used to pay for college and college-related expenses. (Since the law was first enacted in 1996, the definition of *qualified higher education expenses* has been expanded to include more of what a family would typically expect these expenses to be.)

As amended by the Economic Growth and Tax Relief Reconciliation Act of 2001 (EGTRRA), Section 529 Plan distributions, including all investment gains and profits, will be completely free of any tax at the time the money is used if it is withdrawn for one or more of the following:

- tuition;
- room and board (if the student is enrolled at least half-time);
- fees;
- books;
- supplies;
- equipment required for enrollment; or,
- for special needs children—expenses incurred in connection with the child's enrollment or attendance at an eligible school.

✦THE COLLEGE SAVINGS ACCOUNT FUNDS MUST BE USED AT AN "ELIGIBLE EDUCATIONAL INSTITUTION"

Remember that even though the funds in the 529 Plan need to be used for *qualified expenses*, they must also be used at an "eligible educational institution". The law defines the term *eligible education institution* by means of reference to the Higher Education Act of 1965. A simpler definition is that any accredited college or graduate school, or post secondary trade or vocational school that can participate in the federal student aid program will qualify.

It is absolutely imperative that you verify that the school is accredited and eligible under this definition. You can find out by contacting the school directly or by asking the Plan Manager sponsoring the plan in the state in which the school is located. If the school is not accredited and therefore not eligible, then any distributions from a College Savings Account will be fully taxed to the owner of the account and subject to the additional 10% penalty.

FUTURE CHANGES IN THE LAW

Changes to the law are made on a frequent basis-both to the Internal Revenue Code Section, and to any regulations. One item to keep track of is the possibility that the College Savings Plan and its law may *sunset* (come to an end) on December 31, 2010. The *sunset* provision requires additional legislation to keep the College Savings Plan law on the books. Were the law to *sunset* without any changes being implemented, then many of the following will expire on that date:

- tax-free distributions of earnings;
- the ability to rollover plan assets without a change of beneficiary;
- the addition of "first cousin" as a member of the family;
- the ability to contribute to a Coverdell Savings Account (see Chapter 2) in the same year as a contribution is made to a College Savings Account;
- rules about applicability of the College Savings Plan to "special needs" individuals; and,
- the coordination with HOPE Scholarships and Lifetime Learning Credits (see Chapter 2).

While it is unlikely, it is possible that the law will sunset on December 31, 2010. It is *unlikely* as recent estimates put the value of College Savings Accounts at approximately $100 billion by the end of this decade. This will represent a substantial portion of the population that is saving funds for college. For this reason, Congress will be hard pressed to reverse the favorable tax benefits given these College Savings Accounts. (Nonetheless, if these accounts were no longer to be treated with these favorable tax benefits—they *sunset*— then any withdrawal from the accounts, whether used for qualified higher education expenses or not, would be subject to ordinary income tax and possibly the penalty tax of 10%.)

THE 529 PLAN

✦ The 529 Plan, also known as the College Savings Plan, is a state sponsored savings plan to assist families saving for college.

✦ These plans allow for the investments to grow and appreciate on a tax-deferred basis during the years of accumulation.

529 PLAN REQUIREMENTS

✦ The account may only receive cash contributions not stocks, securities, or other business interests.

✦ No one, whether owner, contributor, or beneficiary of a College Savings Plan, can have investment control over the account.

✦ Only certain maximum levels of funding of a College Plan Account are allowed for a particular beneficiary.

✦ College Savings Account cannot be pledged as collateral or security.

✦ The program as administered by the states must provide a separate accounting for each beneficiary.

✦ The College Savings Account must be used for qualified higher education expenses to receive favorable tax benefits.

HELPING TO SAVE
FOR COLLEGE

Any discussion of saving for college should begin with a clear understanding of the goals you are trying to achieve. As most financial and estate planners will tell you, it is the mere fact that you have a plan that separates you from the pack. Developing a plan of attack is the place to begin. To do this, we must first calculate the amount that is needed to put a child through college. For simplicity sake, we will focus our discussion on the use of College Savings Plan assets for payment of college expenses. Remember, these College Savings accounts can be used for payments of expenses at post-secondary educational institutions which offer credits towards a:

- bachelors degree;
- associates degree;
- graduate level or professional degree; or,
- other recognized post-secondary credential.

This means that whether the student is attending a community college, a vocational school, or a graduate school, the assets in the College Savings Plan can be used to pay those expenses and receive the favorable tax benefits.

The following two tables provide an estimate of cost for several colleges across the country. This first one relates the 2001–2002 school year expenses, and the second one relates the estimated expenses in the 2010–2011 school year. This should give you some sense of the current reality that confronts families saving for college expenses.

COST OF COLLEGE
2001-2002 ANNUAL EXPENSES

College	Tuition	Room & Board	Fees, Books & Supplies	Total
Columbia University	$25,000	$8,000	$ 3,000	$36,000
Harvard University	$ 26,000	$8,000	$ 2,000	$36,000
Kansas State University (non-resident)	$9,000	$5,000	$3,000	$17,000
Stevens Institute of Technology	$22,000	$5,000	$2,000	$27,000

COST OF COLLEGE
2010-2011 ANNUAL EXPENSES
(ESTIMATED 6% INCREASE)

College	Tuition	Room & Board	Fees, Books & Supplies	Total
Columbia University	$43,000	$13,000	$5,000	$61,000
Harvard University	$44,000	$13,000	$3,000	$62,000
Kansas State University (non-resident)	$15,000	$8,500	$5,000	$28,500
Stevens Institute of Technology	$35,000	$8,500	$3,500	$47,000

What this tells us is that the sooner a family begins to invest for college—the better. In fact, as the following table illustrates, the sooner you start the greater the likelihood of reaching the funding levels you need.

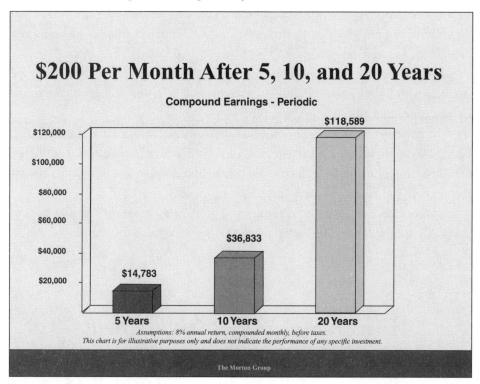

$200 Per Month After 5, 10, and 20 Years

Compound Earnings - Periodic

Assumptions: 8% annual return, compounded monthly, before taxes.
This chart is for illustrative purposes only and does not indicate the performance of any specific investment.

The Morton Group

NOTE: *While the College Savings Plan is scheduled to sunset on December 31, 2010, most commentators and planners envision this College Savings Plan extending beyond the possible sunset year.*

TAXES AND TAX DEFERRED SAVINGS

The effect that income taxes have on long-term savings plans can never be understated. The combination of federal, and where applicable, state income taxes on investments can prevent investments from growing as quickly as we would like. The drain that these taxes can have on investment returns can often be substantial. Certainly, the higher the income tax bracket the more severe the affect income taxes have on the growth of the savings or *portfolio*. For this reason it has long been understood that tax-deferred investing is preferred over taxable investing.

Prior to the beginning of the Coverdell Savings Account and the College Savings Plan, the only traditional investments that were tax-deferred, in nature, were retirement plans (pension plans, profit sharing plans, defined benefit plans, 401(k)'s, individual retirement accounts, etc.) and annuities. (The Coverdell Savings Account is discussed on pages 22–25.) Since retirement accounts are intended for retirement, federal laws have established a minimum age of 59 before withdrawals can be made. This same age rule applies to *annuities* sold by insurance companies. In both these cases, the early withdrawal from the account or the annuity will result in some level of income taxation.

The tax deferral opportunity presented by College Savings Plans and Coverdell Savings Accounts, when compared to traditional taxable investments, is substantial. The following table illustrates the difference on a 5, 10 and 20-year time-line when investing tax-deferred versus investing in a taxable account:

It is clear that tax-deferred investing will more often generate a greater pool of assets when compared to the same assets growing in a taxable account.

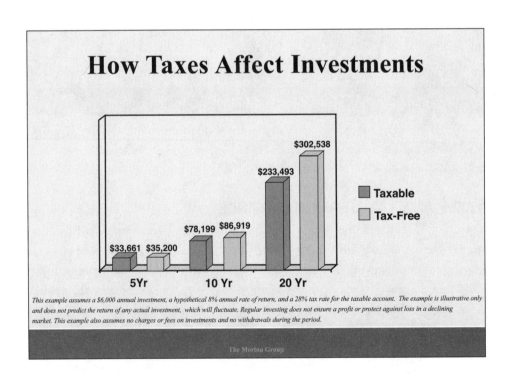

How Taxes Affect Investments

This example assumes a $6,000 annual investment, a hypothetical 8% annual rate of return, and a 28% tax rate for the taxable account. The example is illustrative only and does not predict the return of any actual investment, which will fluctuate. Regular investing does not ensure a profit or protect against loss in a declining market. This example also assumes no charges or fees on investments and no withdrawals during the period.

The Morton Group

COLLEGE SAVINGS ACCOUNTS VERSUS OTHER METHODS OF SAVING FOR COLLEGE

To truly understand and appreciate the unique opportunity afforded by the College Savings Plan, you should have a working knowledge of the alternative ways to save money for college. The most popular choices follow.

✦CUSTODIAL ACCOUNTS

A *custodial account* is one in which a person (the *custodian*) holds money or other investments for the benefit of a person not yet of *full age* and *legal capacity*, usually age 18 or 21. The person who is responsible for holding the assets is known as the *custodian*. These accounts are commonly referred to as UGMA Accounts (accounts created under the Uniform Gifts to Minors Act) or as UTMA Accounts (accounts created under the Uniform Transfers to Minors Act). In either case the approach is the same. An account is created for someone who is typically under the age of 18 or in some cases under the age of 21. The custodian is in charge of all investment decisions, decisions about use of money, and any necessary distributions.

Income earned in these types of accounts is taxable to the child for whom the account is established. Under the "Kiddie Tax" rules, all income earned in this type of an account for a child under the age of 14 is taxable to the parent, at the parent's highest income tax bracket. Income earned in these types of accounts are fully taxable to the child, on the child's personal income tax return at the child's income tax rate, once the child is over the age of 14.

Benefits of a Custodial Account

1. No loss of control over investments. The investments are fully under the control of the custodian (typically the parent of the child for whom the account was established). Therefore, the assets can be invested in any type of investment the custodian selects. Certainly the custodian has a duty to make the assets productive without taking unnecessary risk. However, within the boundaries of reason, the custodian has a fair amount of latitude. The flexibility of investments for these accounts allow a custodian to invest in certificates of deposits, stocks, bonds, real estate and mutual funds. Typically the investment latitude does not extend to investments in or the trading of *options* (buying or selling stocks a fixed price).

2. *Tax Savings.* Because the child will receive a standard deduction of $500 *and* an itemized deduction of $500, the first $1,000 of income completely escapes any form of taxation at the federal level. This is certainly an advantage over investing these same assets in a taxable joint account owned by the parents. (In cases where the assets are invested in a taxable joint account by the parents, there is no special $500 standard deduction or $500 itemized deduction to protect these taxable investments.)

3. *Ease of Administration.* Opening and maintaining a UGMA/UTMA custodial account is normally very easy. There is typically just an account opening form to begin the process. The account is maintained in the same fashion as any other savings or investment account would be maintained.

Disadvantages of Custodial Accounts

1. *Mandatory Required Distribution.* The laws of the state that you reside in will require the complete distribution of assets in a UGMA/UTMA custodial account when the child for whom the account has been established reaches age 18 or in some cases 21. In either case, this mandatory distribution is the single greatest problem with UGMA/UTMA custodial accounts. To the extent there are assets left in an account, whether as a result of the child not going to college, or a child receiving a scholarship or other financial aid, the remaining assets must be distributed to the child at the age stipulated by your state's laws. This can be problematic if a child is struggling with alcohol, gambling or drug abuse at these same ages.

2. *Custodial Accounts create ownership rights.* Custodial accounts by their nature are accounts owned by the child, but under the control of someone else—the custodian. These accounts really do belong to the child. For this reason, any inappropriate use of the money, or any steps to make the funds unreachable at the age of distribution is likely to violate state law. This can allow the child to sue or take other legal action against the custodian.

For example:

Mary creates a UGMA account under Illinois' laws. The account is for the benefit of her son, Phillip, age 9. Allen, Phillip's father, is named as the custodian of the account. Under Illinois' laws, the account must be turned over to the child at age 18. When Phillip is 17 years old, the account has a total value of $100,000 which Mary and Allen intended to use for Phillip's college expense. Unfortunately, Phillip is involved with alcohol and drugs and does not intend to go to college. He is looking forward to his 18th birthday when Allen will be turning over the UGMA account.

To prevent Phillip from getting the money, Allen transfers the entire UGMA account to an *irrevocable trust* (can never be changed) controlled by Allen himself. The trust provides that all of the assets are for Phillip's benefit, but that Phillip cannot have the principal distributed outright to him until he reaches age 35. This transfer to the trust to gain greater control over the assets may violate the state's UGMA law, as it prevented Phillip from gaining control at age 18. Phillip's recourse is to file suit against Allen for the wrongful transfer of assets away from Phillip's control.

NOTE: *Be careful. This often happens as families struggle to determine the right thing to do when the wrong thing is happening to their family.*

3. *Taxation.* An account that has grown in size will begin to generate income that will be fully taxable to the child (or the parent under the "Kiddie Tax"). This taxation on the investment income will stunt the growth of the assets. This taxable nature of the account, when compared to the ability to invest on a tax-deferred basis, is a true disadvantage of the UTMA/UGMA account. (See the table on page 18 for a comparison of taxable versus tax-deferred investment returns.)

4. *Estate Taxation.* One side benefit to many gift-giving programs is that the gift, once made, is removed from the gift giver's estate for estate tax purposes. This means that each time a gift is made into a UGMA/UTMA account the amount of the gift is no longer taxable to the person making

the gift. Unfortunately, this desire to remove the assets from the gift giver's estate does not always occur. Depending on the formalities of the establishment and maintenance of a UGMA/UTMA custodian account, the funds in the account may be included in the estate of the person who is making the gift and remain fully taxable.

Estate tax and gift tax law are clear. If you make a gift, but then control the gift after having made it, the assets never really leave your ownership and the account is fully taxable in your estate should you pass away. To avoid this problem, the custodian of the account should not be the same person that is making the gifts into the account.

> For example:
> Sally creates a UGMA account under Illinois' laws. The account is for the benefit of her son, Mickey, age 9. Sally doesn't trust George, Mickey's father, to properly handle the investments, and so Sally sets up the account and names herself as the custodian. Each year Sally makes a contribution to the account. Several years later, when the account has grown in size, Sally dies. Since she continued to control the account at her death and was the person making the annual gifts, the account should be included in Sally's taxable estate for estate tax purposes. This could have been avoided if she either named George as the custodian, or even if she had remained custodian, by merely having George make the annual gifts. ■

✦Coverdell Education Savings Accounts ("Education IRA's)

The *Coverdell Education Savings Account* (often referred to as an "Education IRA") is a savings or investment account into which parents can contribute a maximum of $2,000 per year as of calendar year 2002. The investments have the opportunity to grow tax-deferred. When the funds are withdrawn for qualified education expenses, including primary and secondary education expenses as well as college expenses, the withdrawals, and all increases and gains in the account are completely tax-free.

The investments a parent can make in a Coverdell Savings Account are completely under the control of the person who establishes the account. The assets can be invested in the most common of investments such as stocks, bonds, mutual funds and certificates of deposit. For families that can save a maximum of $2,000 per year per child, the Coverdell Savings Account may most likely be the best choice available.

Requirements of a Coverdell Savings Account

To qualify for the establishment and for the right to contribute to a Coverdell Savings Account, there are certain income limitations. To qualify, a married couple must have an *adjusted gross income* (on their income tax return—Form 1040) of $190,000 or less. As the income grows from $190,000 to $220,000 the ability to contribute to an Education IRA is phased out and cannot be done. For single taxpayers, the income limit is $95,000, again being phased out at $110,000. Furthermore, contributions for a given tax year must be made on or before April 15th of the following year.

NOTE: *Assets in the Coverdell Savings Account (Education IRA) must be used for qualified education expenses (including qualified elementary and secondary school expenses, as well as college and graduate school) or must be rolled over to another beneficiary before the original beneficiary turns age 30.*

For example:

In 2002, Nicole (who is single and has an adjusted gross income of $60,000) establishes a Coverdell Savings Account for the benefit of her son, Steven, age 15. Steven ends up attending college, but not until he is age 25. He graduates from college at age 29, with $600 remaining in the Coverdell Education IRA Account. Nicole can name her second son, Jay, age 14, attending a private high school, as the beneficiary of the account and avoid any penalty for failure to use the account assets before Steven turns age 30. Now Jay can withdraw the funds in the account, and if used for qualified education expenses, any gain on the assets will be completely tax-free. ■

Benefits of a Coverdell Savings Account

1. *No loss of control over investments.* As the investments are fully under the control of the creator of the account (typically the parent of the child for whom the account was established), the assets are invested in any type of investment the owner selects. Certainly there is a duty to make the investments grow without taking unnecessary risk, but within the boundaries of reason, the owner has a fair amount of latitude. The flexibility of investments for these accounts allow the owner to invest in certificates of deposits, stocks, bonds, real estate and mutual funds. (These investments can contain some amount of risk, including loss of principle.) Typically the investment latitude does not extend to investments in or the trading of options.

2. *Contributions can be made by anyone.* As long as the person making the contribution meets the income tests, the person can contribute to an existing Education IRA for the benefit of anyone they choose—provided the beneficiary is under age 18. An exception to this age limitation exists for special needs individuals, for whom contributions can be made even after age 18.

3. *Tax Deferral/Tax Free Withdrawal.* Much like the benefits of investing within a qualified retirement plan, an individual retirement account (i.e. a 401(K)), or a College Savings Account, the assets in a Coverdell Savings Account grow on a tax-deferred basis. If the assets are used for qualified education expenses (including primary and secondary education expenses as of 2002), then all gains are completely tax-free.

4. *Ease of Administration.* Opening and maintaining a Coverdell Savings Account are normally very easy. There is typically an account opening form to begin the process. The account is then maintained in the same fashion as any other savings or investment account would be maintained.

5. *Account Transferability.* The Education IRA Account is transferable. A parent can transfer the account to another child should the child for whom it was originally established elect not to attend college, or does not utilize all of the assets for college.

Disadvantages of Coverdell Savings Accounts

1. *Mandatory Required Distribution.* The law mandates that all assets in the account be utilized before the original beneficiary's 30th birthday. The law does allow for the naming of a new beneficiary, but this age restriction of the original beneficiary continues to apply.

2. *Income Limitations on Funding.* By limiting the ability to contribute to an Education IRA based upon a person's earnings (adjusted gross income), the Education IRA discriminates against those who earn higher income. It *phases out* the benefit of the Education IRA based upon certain adjusted income levels. When a family's income exceeds the allowable amount, the Education IRA and its benefits are no longer allowed.

3. *Contribution Limitations.* Because the contribution limit is currently $2,000 per year, it will be difficult to grow the substantial funds necessary to satisfy the anticipated expense of college. In addition, some families may qualify for the funding of a Coverdell Account in the early years of saving for college, but not qualify, due to adjusted gross income limitations, in later years. This will limit the pool of assets growing in the account.

4. *Gift/Estate Taxes.* The assets in a Coverdell Savings Account are considered the assets of the account owner. For this reason there is no completed gift to remove the assets from the owners estate. Therefore, the full value of the account will be included in the taxable estate of the account owner should he or she die while the account is funded.

✦PREPAID TUITION PLANS

The *Prepaid Tuition Plan* established by a state allows for the purchase of tuition credits (like class credits when attending college) for use at participating colleges, typically within the state's borders. These credits are held until the child attends college and are then redeemed for the number of credits purchased. Regardless of how much more the tuition is at the time of redemption, the credits purchased long ago are used as full payment of the current tuition. However, the credits *must* be used at a participating college.

Benefits of a Prepaid Tuition Plan

1. *Guarantee of Sufficient Savings.* The Prepaid Tuition Plan affords the owner the guarantee that the number of credits purchased will be redeemed for the same number of fully paid credits when the child attends college. This is a substantial advantage over traditional savings for college. The fluctuations in investment returns and the increasing cost of education may keep the savings from being sufficient when needed. By purchasing a guarantee (as the Prepaid Tuition Plan affords), the account owner has eliminated a large risk factor in saving sufficient funds for college.

2. *Contributions can be made by anyone.* Any person can purchase Prepaid Tuition for the benefit of anyone they choose.

3. *Tax Deferral/Tax Free Withdrawal.* Much like the benefits of investing within a qualified retirement plan, an individual retirement account, or a College Savings Plan, the Prepaid Tuition Plan assets grow on a tax-deferred basis. If the tuition plan assets are used for qualified higher education expenses, then all gains are completely tax-free.

4. *Ease of Administration.* Purchasing the Prepaid Tuition Plan credits is a relatively simple matter. Most states have established these accounts with financial services institutions to make the purchase a simple transaction.

Disadvantages of Prepaid Tuition Plans

1. *Typically Applies to Schools within the State.* Many states establish the plans in coordination with the higher education institutions in that state. Since the premise is that the cost of a college credit can be quantified today and purchased today for use in the future, the state needs to have a good estimate of these costs. For this reason, most states limit the use of the prepaid tuition to schools within the state.

2. *Fixed or Low Rates of Return.* Students may wish to attend schools in other states. Therefore, most Prepaid Tuition Plans have a formula for calculating the amount to be returned to the owner should the student elect to attend school at an institution that does not honor the credits, or in a state that does not meet with the terms of the plan. Very often the amount of interest paid on these refunded prepaid tuition plan dollars is very small.

3. *Penalty for Nonqualified Withdrawal.* Most plans provide for a penalty should the prepaid plan be terminated for use other than for qualified higher education expenses.

◆PRIVATE/FAMILY CREATED COLLEGE SAVINGS TRUSTS

Traditionally there have been several commonly used forms of *irrevocable trusts* (trusts that once created, can never be changed again) used for the purpose of saving funds for college. In general, a parent or grandparent would meet with their estate planner to discuss the use of some form of a trust to receive and manage assets being saved for college. In every case where an irrevocable (unchangeable) trust was put in place, the person making the gift transfers the assets into the irrevocable trust. Once the assets were in the trust, the person who made the gift no longer had any form of control over the assets. Furthermore, there was no ability to change a beneficiary of the trust or expand the class of people who might benefit from the trust's assets.

Some versions of the irrevocable trust follow.

Section 2503(c) trusts

The *Section 2503(c) trust*, a trust specially created by tax law, allows for the saving of assets in an irrevocable trust, with all income earned being kept in the trust. The trust pays all income tax on the earnings at the trust's income tax rate. By virtue of tax law changes a number of years ago, the income tax on a trust's income is very high after a modest level of income has been earned. When the child attains age 21 the trustee (the person in charge of following the rules of the trust) must distribute the remaining trust assets outright to the child. This age 21 termination, along with the high level of income tax, has caused these types of trust to fall out of favor as a means to save for college.

Section 2503(b) trusts

The *Section 2503(b) trust*, another type created by law, allows for the saving of assets in an irrevocable trust, with all income earned being distributed to the child. The child pays all income tax on the earnings at the child's or parents' income tax rate, depending on the age of the child. When the child reaches age 25, the trustee must distribute the remaining trust assets outright to the child. This age 25 termination, along with the high level of income tax until the child reaches age 14 (the "Kiddie Tax" issues) has caused these types of trusts to fall out of favor as a means to saving for college as well.

Crummey Trusts

Crummey type irrevocable trusts allow for greater control over the principal of the trust for a longer period of time. In these types of trusts the creator of the trust can stipulate at the time of creation how old a child must be to receive the trust principal. The problem with this type of trust is that the child must receive notice of each gift of assets to the trust, and the child is afforded a certain amount of time (typically not less than 30 days) to remove the gift from the trust. The assets that do remain in the trust are typically taxed to the trust at the trust's very high income tax rates. Required notification at the time of each gift, along with the high income tax burden on these trusts has caused these types of trusts to fall out of favor as a means to save for college as well.

COLLEGE SAVINGS PLAN/SECTION 529 ADVANTAGE

The key to the College Savings Plan is that the investments and savings grow without having any tax imposed on them. This type of investment without taxation is often referred to as tax-deferred investing. Regardless of what tax is or is not imposed at the time the money is withdrawn, the growth on the investments during all of the years prior to withdrawal is on this tax-deferred basis. The advantages of tax-deferred growth are substantial. No matter the tax bracket you are in, you may achieve greater savings when you do not have to reduce your gains (i.e. interest) by an income tax (federal and state).

Unlike the traditional savings plan where all income earned is taxed in the year the income is generated, with the College Savings Plan you have the potential to grow the money that would have been sent to the tax collector.

Taking advantage of tax-deferred growth whenever possible makes great investment sense. This is the very same reason many people try to fully fund their retirement plans (individual retirement accounts, 401(k)'s, etc.) to take advantage of the tax-deferred growth on their investments afforded by the qualified retirement plan. This tax-deferred growth is the very same reason that the College Savings Plan, with its tax-deferred growth, provides a wonderful advantage to a family trying to save and grow assets for college.

As is discussed in Chapter 4, the College Savings Plan also allows for an unprecedented amount of control by the creator of the account over the eventual use of the assets. While direct control over the nature of the investments is prohibited, the owner or creator has control over when the assets are used and for whom they are used. This provides substantial estate planning opportunities that previously have not existed. The ability to change the beneficiary allows for the redirection of assets from one beneficiary to another if the assets are not needed or are not used for college. This also allows for saving money for college before children are even born, or to save for grandchildren that are years away from being born.

COORDINATION OF HOPE SCHOLARSHIP CREDIT WITH SECTION 529 COLLEGE SAVINGS PLANS

The Hope and Lifetime Learning Credits (education credits) afford a tax credit to families who meet certain income levels. The Hope Scholarship Credit is a maximum credit of $1,500 per student each calendar year. The Lifetime Learning Credit can be a maximum of $2,000 in calendar year 2002. Recent tax laws allow for the education credits to be taken in a year when withdrawals are made from a 529 Plan for the very same beneficiary. If the 529 Plan withdrawals are made and used for the same expenses as the education credits, then the withdrawal from the Section 529 Plan will not be tax free. The law requires that the qualified higher education expenses for Section 529 be reduced by expenses used whether a Hope or Lifetime Learning Credit is available.

Chapter 2

At a Glance

UNDERSTANDING IS THE FIRST STEP

✦ The cost of college is out-pacing inflation.

✦ It is important to find ways to save for college that will provide the best possible return with the least amount of taxation along the way.

TAXABLE VERSUS TAX-DEFERRED

✦ The growth comparison of taxable investments versus tax deferred investments shows that the ability to defer the income tax burden on investment gains allows for the invested assets to grow more rapidly.

✦ Where possible, look for tax-deferred methods of growing assets rather than taxable forms of investing.

CHOICES AVAILABLE FOR SAVING FOR COLLEGE:

CUSTODIAL ACCOUNTS (ALSO KNOWN AS UTMA OR UGMA ACCOUNTS)

✦ These accounts are easy to set up and easy to maintain.

✦ These are taxable in nature and require that all assets be distributed at the age stipulated by law (either 18 or 21).

COVERDELL SAVINGS ACCOUNTS (ALSO KNOWN AS EDUCATION IRA's)

✦ These are easy to set up and maintain.

✦ The benefit is phased out for individuals/families with adjusted gross income above certain levels.

✦ For families who can save a maximum of $2,000 per year, per child, this is most likely the preferable choice to make.

✦ Assets remain under the control of the account creator and grow tax-deferred and are tax free if used for higher education expenses.

PREPAID TUITION PLANS

✦ These are easy to set up and maintain.

✦ Very often these plans require that the student attend school in the state that sponsored the prepaid plan.

✦ If the student attends school in another state then a refund is offered. (In such a case, the refund carries with it a small growth factor on the investments.)

✦ If the student does attend school in the sponsoring state then all growth on the investment in the plan is tax-free.

FAMILY CREATED TRUSTS

✦ The traditional "education trusts" or "crummey trusts" as created by a family member are irrevocable in nature, and have an onerous income tax burden.

✦ The trusts are inflexible in nature and can be difficult to administer long term.

✦ These types of trust have fallen out of favor as a means to invest for college.

(continued)

COLLEGE SAVINGS PLANS

✦ The College Savings Plan (529 Plans) affords the investor tax-deferred investment, with tax-free withdrawal if the assets are used for qualified higher education expenses.

✦ The plan allows for the account owner to change beneficiaries, allowing the account owner to keep control of the account.

✦ In addition, the assets in the account should avoid all forms of estate and gift taxation.

TAXATION OF COLLEGE SAVINGS PLANS

The College Savings Plan is a creation of federal tax law, specifically Internal Revenue Code Section 529. As with all tax laws, the legislative intention is to motivate people in a particular way by virtue of tax benefits to be realized. The College Savings Plan is no different. The intention in creating the law was to help families save for college in a tax favored way. Doing so provides those who are saving for college an advantage over those people who do not have children or whose children have already attended college.

BASIC TAX RULES

In its simplest terms, if you follow the rules, there are no federal or state income taxes on the investment gains in a College Savings Account during the accumulation or growth of the assets. When assets are withdrawn from the College Savings Account, there may be a tax depending on the reason the assets are withdrawn and what they are used for. Section 529 imposes a federal income tax, and an additional penalty tax, in cases where the tax-free withdrawal rules are not followed. (see Chapter 1, page 4.)

The investments grow tax-deferred, and if used for the appropriate *qualified higher education expenses*, the growth on the investments will be tax-free. (See page 10 for an explanation of qualified higher education expenses.)

For example:
In 2002, Mary establishes a College Savings Account under the plan administered by New Jersey's Plan Manager. In 2010, when her son Phillip attends college, there is a total of $30,000 in the College Savings

Account. This represents Mary's contributions over the years of $20,000, and growth on that investment of $10,000. If the account assets are used by Mary for Phillip's qualified higher education expenses, then the $10,000 of growth on the investments will never be taxed. ■

QUALIFIED HIGHER EDUCATION EXPENSES

You must use the funds withdrawn from the College Savings Plan for *qualified higher education expenses* in order to have tax-free investment gains. The basic premise to the plan is that the money saved in this tax-favored savings account is intended to be used to pay for college and college related expenses. Since the law was first enacted in 1996, the definition of *qualified higher education expenses* has been expanded to include more of what a family would typically expect these expenses to be.

As amended by the Economic Growth and Tax Relief Reconciliation of 2001 (EGTRRA), Section 529 College Savings Plan distributions, including all gains and appreciation, are federally tax-free at the time of distribution if used for one or more of the following:

- tuition;
- room and board (if the student is enrolled at least half-time);
- fees;
- books;
- supplies;
- equipment required for enrollment; and,
- for special needs children—expenses incurred in connection with the child's enrollment or attendance at an eligible school.

This list has been expanding and may well include in the future necessary *incidentals* of attending college, such as an automobile to commute to school.

ELIGIBLE INSTITUTION

The funds withdrawn from a College Savings Plan must be used for one or more of the previously mentioned educational expenses, as well as used at an eligible educational institution. An *eligible educational institution* is defined in the Higher Education Act of 1965, as being a school eligible to participate in a student aid program. Generally speaking, these are accredited schools offering credits towards a bachelor's degree, an associates degree, professional, vocational or other post secondary education, such as medical school, law school, and pursuit of doctoral degrees.

■ *The example is provided for informational purposes only and does not reflect the actual performance of any investment. All programs involve investment risk, including the loss of principle. State taxes may be applicable.*

TAXES ON DISTRIBUTIONS

By virtue of tax law changes implemented in 2002, distributions from a College Savings Plan are free from federal income tax provided the distribution is used for payment of *qualified higher education expenses*. This then raises the question of what taxes are to be paid if the withdrawal is not for the higher education expenses. That is, what if a withdrawal is made from the account and the proceeds are used for some other expense. Under current federal tax law the owner of the account would have to list on his or her income tax return the amount of the distribution that was made up of gains and investment profits. The income portion of this distribution would then be subject to income taxes and a penalty tax.

For example:

In 1999, Sally opened a College Savings Account for the benefit of Mickey and deposited $20,000 into the account. At the close of the year (December 31) in 2006, the account value will be $30,000. If Sally were to withdraw $7,500 from the account and not use the money for qualified higher education expenses for Mickey, then a portion of the withdrawal will be subject to federal income tax. The portion is computed based upon the ratio of income to principal in the account. In this case, the proportion is 2/3 principal 1/3 income. Therefore, one-third of the distribution that was not used for qualified higher education would be subject to income tax. In this example, when Sally withdrew $7,500 from the account, one-third of this, or $2,500, would be put on her income tax return as taxable income. ■

DEDUCTIONS FOR CONTRIBUTIONS – FEDERAL

Under present law there is no deduction on your federal income tax return for contributions to a College Savings Plan. While it may be possible that Congress will take this step in the future, there is no indication at the present time that they will do so. Presently, if you wish to save money for retirement, you can also do so on a *pretax basis*. This is done by using a 401(k), IRA or an employer's pension or profit-sharing plan. These types of plans all allow for you to save money before any income tax is imposed on your earnings. Perhaps Congress will see that this pre-tax savings would be an opportunity for families trying to save for college, and may some day offer a similar tax-deductible way to put money into a College Savings Account.

■ *The example is provided for informational purposes only and does not reflect the actual performance of any investment. All programs involve investment risk, including the loss of principle. State taxes may be applicable.*

DEDUCTIONS FOR CONTRIBUTIONS – STATE

Some states have enacted laws that allow for a partial or complete deduction against state income tax for contributions to a state's home plan. That means that for someone living in a state that allows for a deduction, the contribution to a College Savings Plan will reduce their current state income tax burden each year.

The following is a state-by-state summary of tax deductibility on contributions to a College Savings Plan at the time of this book's publication. There is also a general summary of the income tax structure of the states to help determine the economic value of a potential tax deduction.

State	Deduction for Contribution	Tax Rates High	Low
Alabama	Plan under development	2.0	5.0
Alaska	NO state income tax		
Arizona	NO	2.87	5.04
Arkansas	NO	1.0	7.0
California	NO	1.0	9.3
Colorado	YES unlimited	4.63 flat rate	
Connecticut	NO	3.0	4.5
Delaware	NO	2.2	5.95
Florida	No state income tax		
Georgia	Plan under development	1.0	6.0
Hawaii	Plan under development	1.5	8.5
Idaho	Yes—up to $4,000/year		
Illinois	YES—unlimited	3.0 flat rate	
Indiana	NO	3.4 flat rate	
Iowa	YES $2,112/year/beneficiary	.368	.98
Kansas	YES $2,000/year/beneficiary $4,000/year/beneficiary married filing joint	3.5	6.45
Kentucky	NO	2.0	6.0
Louisiana	YES $2,400/year/beneficiary	2.0	6.0
Maine	NO	2.0	8.5
Maryland	YES $2,500/year/beneficiary	2.0	4.8
Massachusetts	NO	5.6 flat rate	

State	Deduction for Contribution	Tax Rates	
		High	**Low**
Michigan	YES $5,000/year/beneficiary $10,000/year married filing joint	4.2 flat rate	
Minnesota	NO	5.35	7.85
Mississippi	YES $10,000/year $20,000/year married filing joint	3.0	5.0
Missouri	YES $8,000/year/taxpayer	1.5	6.0
Montana	YES $3,000/year $6,000/year married filing joint	2.0	11.0
Nebraska	YES $1,000 maximum	2.51	6.68
Nevada	No state income tax		
New Hampshire	NO	Interest and dividends income tax only	
New Jersey	NO	1.4	6.37
New Mexico	YES unlimited	1.7	8.20
New York	YES $10,000/year $20,000/year married filing joint	4.0	6.85
North Carolina	NO	6.0	7.75
North Dakota	NO	2.67	12.0
Ohio	YES $2,000/year/beneficiary	0.69	16.98
Oklahoma	YES $2,500/year/beneficiary	0.5	6.75
Oregon	YES max $2,000/year/donor	5.0	9.0
Rhode Island	NO	25.5% of federal tax liability	
Tennessee	NO	dividends and income taxed only	
Utah	YES $1,410/year $2,820/year married filing joint	2.3	7.0
Vermont	NO	24% of federal tax liability	
Virginia	YES $2,000/contract/year	2.0	5.75
Washington	NO state income tax		
Wisconsin	YES $3,000/year/beneficiary	4.6	6.75
Wyoming	NO state income tax		
District of Columbia	Plan under development	5.0	9.0

To put this in perspective, consider the following illustrations of the value (or lack of value) in the deductibility of a contribution to a state's home plan.

> For example:
>
> In 2002, Mary, residing in Illinois, establishes a College Savings Account for her son under Illinois' Plan Manager (presently Salomon Smith Barney). Under the state's income tax rules, there is an unlimited income tax deduction when contributions are made to the plan sponsored by the state. In this case, if Mary contributed $20,000 to her son's account there would be a tax savings of $600 ($20,000 times the state's flat income tax rate of 3.0%). ■
>
> In 2002, Sally, a single individual, residing in Mississippi, establishes a College Savings Account for her son under Mississippi's Plan Manager (presently TIAA-CREF). Under the state's income tax rules, there is a limited income tax deduction for contributions up to $10,000 when contributions are made to the plan sponsored by the state. In this case, if Sally was in the highest tax bracket and she contributed $20,000 to her son's account there would be a tax savings of $500 (maximum benefit level of $10,000 times the state's income tax rate of 5.0%). ■
>
> In 2002, Nicole, a single individual, residing in Massachusetts, establishes a College Savings Account under Massachusetts' Plan Manager (presently Fidelity Investments). Under the state's income tax rules, there is no income tax deduction for contributions made to a College Savings Account. In this case, Nicole would receive no state income tax benefit for contributions to the account. ■

You can see that states that offer a state tax deduction for contributions to a College Savings Account save real money for consumers. This is achieved by allowing families to invest money in a College Savings Plan and reducing their current taxable income by the amount of the contribution.

Therefore, it is important to understand the state income tax benefit, if any, of each particular state. When a state provides a valuable tax benefit to use the state's own Plan, the consumer needs to determine the actual economic value/benefit of doing so. As with any investment decision, there are many factors to consider when selecting an appropriate College Savings Plan. Thought must be given to issues of state income tax deductibility for contributions. Also, consider investment performance among the plans, fees and expenses.

For example:

Mary establishes a College Savings Account for her son under the plan administered by an Illinois Plan Manager. Under the state's income tax rules, there is an unlimited income tax deduction when contributions are made to the plan sponsored by the state. In this case, if Mary contributed $10,000 to her son's account there would be a tax savings of $300 ($10,000 times the state's flat income tax rate of 3.0%).

Let's say Mary then reviews the investment choices and returns on investment for the plan sponsored by Illinois. Mary may see that the state's plan has only 5 investment choices, not 10 or more as offered by other states' Plan Managers. In addition, Mary sees that the Illinois plan is under-performing plans managed by other Plan Managers by a wide margin. In this case, Mary may elect to forego the state income tax savings and use a plan offered by a different state.

STATE TAXATION ON WITHDRAWALS FROM A COLLEGE SAVINGS PLAN

The federal law is clear. Withdrawals from a College Savings Plan for use in paying *qualified higher education expenses* are tax-free on the federal level. The same may not be true about taxes that must be paid to the state you reside in. Remember, the College Savings Plan is administered by each state under its own set of rules. As long as the rules the state adopt do not conflict with federal laws, it can establish any rules it likes.

There are many different approaches to state taxation of the College Savings Plan at the time of a withdrawal. The good news is that to the extent there is a tax, the tax burden is charged to the student, at the student's tax rate. The assumption is that the student who is attending college is in a lower income tax bracket then his or her parents would be.

At the present time, a variety of states offer a tax break at the time of withdrawal, including tax-free withdrawal in some cases, if you use the plan sponsored by your home state. Other states have adopted the federal law, which makes all distributions from the state's plan tax-free for anyone, regardless of state residency. There are still other states that have adopted both their own tax-free laws and have adopted the federal laws. This may become important in 2011 when the federal law *sunsets*. Those states that have their own tax-free legislation will continue to allow tax-free withdrawals. States that have only adopted the federal law may become taxable withdrawal states when and if the federal law sunsets.

On the following pages is a summary of the existing state tax rules on distributions from a College Savings Plan maintained under the state's laws at the time of publication of this book.

State	Tax Free Withdrawal?
Alabama	Yes—residents only who use state sponsored plan
Alaska	No State Income Tax
Arizona	Yes—residents and non-residents as well
Arkansas	No State Income Tax
California	No—even residents with state sponsored plan pay tax
Colorado	Yes—residents only who use state sponsored plan
Connecticut	Yes—adopted federal law—tax free withdrawal
Delaware	Yes—adopted federal law—tax free withdrawal
Florida	No state income tax
Georgia	Yes—residents only who use state sponsored plan
Hawaii	No—even residents with state sponsored plan pay tax
Idaho	No- even residents with state sponsored plan pay tax
Illinois	Yes—adopted federal law—tax free withdrawal
Indiana	Yes—residents only who use state sponsored plan
Iowa	Yes—residents only who use state sponsored plan
Kansas	Yes—adopted federal law—tax free withdrawal
Kentucky	Yes—residents only who use state sponsored plan
Louisiana	Yes—adopted federal law—tax free withdrawal
Maine	Yes—adopted federal law—tax free withdrawal
Maryland	Yes—adopted federal law—tax free withdrawal
Massachusetts	No—even residents with state sponsored plan pay tax
Michigan	Yes—adopted federal law—tax free withdrawal
Minnesota	Yes—adopted federal law—tax free withdrawal
Mississippi	Yes—residents only who use state sponsored plan
Missouri	Yes—adopted federal law—tax free withdrawal
Montana	Yes—adopted federal law—tax free withdrawal
Nebraska	Yes—adopted federal law—tax free withdrawal
Nevada	No state income tax
New Hampshire	Yes—residents only who use state sponsored plan
New Jersey	Yes—residents only who use state sponsored plan
New Mexico	Yes—adopted federal law—tax free withdrawal
New York	Yes—adopted federal law—tax free withdrawal
North Carolina	Yes—residents only who use state sponsored plan

State	Tax Free Withdrawal?
North Dakota	Yes—adopted federal law—tax free withdrawal
Ohio	Yes—adopted federal law—tax free withdrawal
Oklahoma	Yes—adopted federal law—tax free withdrawal
Oregon	Yes—adopted federal law—tax free withdrawal
Rhode Island	Yes—adopted federal law—tax free withdrawal
Tennessee	Yes—residents only who use state sponsored plan
Utah	Yes—adopted federal law—tax free withdrawal
Vermont	Yes—adopted federal law—tax free withdrawal
Virginia	Yes—adopted federal law—tax free withdrawal
Washington	No state income tax
Wisconsin	Yes—residents only who use state sponsored plan
Wyoming	No state income tax

It appears from this list, that most states will afford an income tax break at the time of withdrawal. There are a few states that tax both residents and non-residents, and these states' plans must be reviewed carefully to determine whether the income tax at the state level will cause an unnecessary drain on the College Savings Plan proceeds. (We recommend that a a tax professional be consulted before making any investment decisions.)

Another word of caution—some of these states allow for both the state's residents to be tax-free, as well as non-residents to be tax free due to the state's conformity with federal law. There is a concern that those states that have adopted federal law without their own state exemption for residents, may see that federal law sunset in 2011. As of the date of publication, the most generous states are Arizona, Colorado and New Jersey as these states exempt their own residents as well as non-residents.

What all of this should highlight is that not all College Savings Plans are the same. In selecting an appropriate plan for your family thought must be given to issues of taxation and more specifically issues of state income taxes. Many investors and advisors will focus on the risk tolerance and state tax deductibility of contributions, but the analysis should also include an understanding of the state taxation of *withdrawals* from the College Savings Plan.

Chapter 3

At a Glance

BASIC TAX RULES

✦ College Savings Plans afford families and opportunity to invest assets for college on a tax-deferred basis.

✦ When assets are withdrawn from a college savings account the investment gains will be tax-free if the withdrawal is used for *qualified higher education expenses*.

QUALIFIED HIGHER EDUCATION EXPENSES

✦ Qualified higher education expenses include:
  • tuition;
  • room and board;
  • fees;
  • books;
  • supplies;
  • equipment; and,
  • expenses incurred in special needs education.

ELIGIBLE INSTITUTIONS

✦ Eligible institutions include: most colleges and graduate schools or vocational and trade schools that are eligible to participate in federal student aid programs.

(continued)

DEDUCTION FOR CONTRIBUTIONS

✦ *Federal deductions.* There are no federal deductions available for contributions to College Savings Plans.

✦ *State Deductions.* Many of the states provide an income tax benefit/ deduction for contributions made by a resident into the state's home plan. These vary on a state by state basis.

STATE TAXATION

✦ Each state has its own income tax rules some of which do not coordinate with federal tax law.

✦ Some states tax distributions from College Savings Plans.

✦ Some states specifically adopt federal law and have no tax on distributions.

✦ Some other states have no specific law on point. However, they do not have any state income tax.

BENEFICIARY PLANNING

One of the most flexible components of the College Savings Plan is the ability to change the beneficiary of an account from time to time. The following material will outline the basic components to selecting and maintaining a beneficiary of a 529 College Savings Plan as well as some creative planning opportunities.

THE BASICS

Internal Revenue Code Section 529 allows for the establishment of a College Savings Account for purpose of meeting the qualified higher education expenses of the designated beneficiary of the account. Code Section 529, in part, provides, that a designated beneficiary means:

"(A) the individual designated at the commencement of participation in the qualified tuition program as the beneficiary of amounts paid (or to be paid) to the program,

(B) in the case of a change in beneficiaries...the individual who is the new beneficiary..."

This means that any person may be a beneficiary of a College Savings Account. The individual does not need to be a child, a relative, or have any other traditional connection to the account creator/owner. In fact, under many state's plans it is permissible to name a spouse or the account owner's self as the beneficiary of the account.

The College Savings Plan also allows for the change of beneficiary on an account at anytime, and will allow the changes to be free of any taxation or penalty provided certain "family member" rules are followed.

One great uncertainty facing each person saving for a child's college expenses is the question of "what to do if the child does not attend college." The College Savings Plan affords a flexibility to redirect assets to another child or relative that will be attending college. This ability to change the beneficiary of an account is a key component of the College Savings Plan.

If the savings account is in the form of a traditional taxable savings account, then the owner of the account can simply save the money for some other need. If the account was established in the form of a custodial (i.e. UTMA/UGMA) account, then regardless of whether the child attends college or not, the assets in the account belong to the child. (see Chapter 2.) The inability to change the beneficiary of a custodial account is perhaps the greatest negative to opening such an account.

A true advantage of the College Savings Account compared with other types of savings vehicles for College, can be seen when undertaking financial planning with young families. Consider the young married couple planning on having children in the next several years. Basic financial planning tells us that the sooner assets are invested on a tax-deferred basis, the greater the potential growth opportunity. Under the "old" style UTMA/UGMA (see Chapter 2) approach to saving for college, no account could be established until a child was born.

With the College Savings Account, this young couple could establish several College Savings Accounts, naming each other, or themselves, as beneficiaries, and begin the tax-deferred savings. As will be discussed below, the beneficiary of the account can be changed to name a newborn child at some point down the road. This is the first time that a tax-deferred investment account for a child not yet born can be established. Once again, there may be a substantial difference achieved merely by starting sooner.

CHANGING THE BENEFICIARY

The single most frequently asked question, leads to one of the greatest elements of the Section 529 College Savings Plan. "What if my child does not go to college?" is a fair and reasonable question. The College Savings Plan allows for virtually complete control by the owner over who will benefit from the College Savings Account, and when. Again, by allowing the owner of the account the ability to change beneficiaries of the account at anytime affords the College Savings Plan one of its greatest advantages over other forms of saving for college.

✦BENEFICIARY CHANGES— HOW OFTEN AND WITH WHAT IMPACT

One interesting detail about establishing a College Savings Account is that you do not need to tell the beneficiary that you have established the account for him or her. This allows for complete privacy in the matter of selecting and possibly changing your desired beneficiary. For many reasons, including a child who does not end up attending college, the owner of the account may wish to change the beneficiary of the account from time to time. The rules allow for the owner of the account to change the beneficiary at any time he or she wants.

✦HOW TO CHANGE THE BENEFICIARY

Changing the beneficiary on a College Savings Account is extremely easy. The Plan Managers all have a form of a standard Beneficiary Change Form that can be used to revise a beneficiary designation. Completing the form and filing it with the Plan Manager is all that is required. As with all beneficiary designations, it makes good sense to keep a copy of what you filed. It is also sensible to ask the Plan Manager to send you a copy of the beneficiary designation at least once a year to confirm that the Plan Manager has the correct information.

✦FREQUENCY OF CHANGING THE BENEFICIARY

The rules allow you to change the beneficiary of the College Savings Account any time you like. The problem though is that you may cause the account to be taxed, or in some cases, taxed and penalized, if you change the beneficiary to a person who doesn't qualify for tax-free beneficiary changes. To qualify for a tax-free, penalty-free change of beneficiary of an account, the new beneficiary must fall into a "member of the family" class of individuals of the old beneficiary.

✦TAX-FREE BENEFICIARY CHANGES— "MEMBER OF THE FAMILY"

Recent tax law changes expanded the definition of *member of the family* so that any of the individuals on the following list qualify for tax-free, penalty-free change in beneficiary. Remember, when trying to determine whether a new beneficiary falls within one of the relationships listed in this list, you must measure from the *old beneficiary*, not the account owner. This means, if a child is named as the original beneficiary of a College Savings Plan, and the parent decides to make a change to the beneficiary, then the new beneficiary must be a relation of the child (the old beneficiary).

For example:
Sam sets up a College Savings Account for his best friend's daughter, Kim. Kim decides not to go to college, and starts a family of her own. Sam can change the beneficiary to Kim's child, tax-free. ■

The following is a list of relations:
- son son or daughter, or a descendant of either;
- stepson or stepdaughter;
- brother, sister, stepbrother or stepsister;
- father or mother, or ancestor of either;
- stepfather or stepmother;
- son or daughter of a brother or sister (nephews/nieces);
- brother or sister of a mother or father (aunt/uncle);
- son-in-law or daughter-in-law;
- mother-in-law or father-in-law;
- brother-in-law or sister-in-law;
- spouse of any of the above; or,
- the beneficiary's first cousin.

For example:
Mary established a College Savings Account for the benefit of her son, Phillip, age 15. At age 18, Phillip decides to travel the world rather than attend college. Mary obtains a change of beneficiary designation form from the Plan Manager and names her daughter, Michelle, age 13 as the new College Savings Plan beneficiary. This qualifies as a tax-free change of beneficiary as Michelle is a "member of the family" in relation to Phillip. ■

In the same example, Mary could name a nephew or niece as beneficiary if she chose to and this would also qualify as a tax-free change of beneficiary. ■

In the same example, if Mary, as the account owner, names a person who is not related to Phillip (the original beneficiary), then the change in beneficiary would not be tax-free. If Mary named the son of her next door neighbor as beneficiary, then such a change would force the College Savings Plan to be taxed and Mary would also, as the account owner, have to pay a penalty tax of 10% of the income of the account.

✦Maximum Contribution Limits and Changes to Existing Plans

It is important to remember when changing a beneficiary on a College Savings Account that the total amount set aside for that beneficiary cannot exceed the maximum contribution limit for that beneficiary. As you may recall, each state establishes the maximum amount that may be set aside for a child's higher education expenses. Exceeding this limit may result in an unnecessary income tax and penalty. The Plan Manager will have a procedure to alert you to any excess contribution.

In addition, most Plan Managers will ask that you sign a statement that the total of all College Savings Account's for the beneficiary do not exceed the maximum contribution limit. It is important then to be certain you know the limits in your state to avoid any surprises. The state-by-state plan summary in Appendix B provides a state-by-state detail of maximum contribution levels.

For example:

Sally established a College Savings Account for the benefit of her son, Mickey, age 15. At age 18 Mickey decides to travel the world rather than attend college. Sally obtains a change of beneficiary designation form from the Plan Manager and names her daughter, Alexia, age 13 as the new College Savings Plan beneficiary. The account at that time has a total value of $200,000.

On the date that Sally names Alexia as the beneficiary of the account, Alexia had a separate College Savings Account with a total of $75,000 of asset value. The State in which Sally resides has established a maximum contribution limit of $232,000 for the year in which the beneficiary change was to be made.

This change of beneficiary designation to Alexia exceeds the maximum contribution limit by $43,000 ($200,000 + $75,000=$275,000, and $275,000-$232,000=$43,000). So, the Plan Manager will have to refuse the excess contribution. If the Plan Manager did not refuse the addition, then the change of beneficiary would not qualify in total as a tax-free change, and would subject the excess contributions ($43,000) to tax and penalty. ■

MAKING CHANGES TO AN EXISTING COLLEGE SAVINGS PLAN

As the Plan Managers begin to gain some experience managing the assets in these College Savings Plans, changes will occur. Some Plan Managers may develop a certain style or investment strategy, while other Plan Managers may offer limited investment options. Fees, expenses, fund options, state tax issues which can change overnight, dictate that the consumer have the right to change Plan Managers if needed. Here are the choices.

◆TAX-FREE CHANGES

Section 529 allows for tax-free changes to your College Savings Plan if one of the following happens within sixty (60) days of any of the following changes:

1. *Change of Plan Manager for the benefit of the same beneficiary.* The rules allow you to change from one Plan Manager to another, provided that the account opened with the new Plan Manager is for the same designated beneficiary. This change of Plan Managers, perhaps in an effort to secure better investment performance or to secure a state income tax deduction for contributions, requires that this change occur only once per year. Any change of Plan Manager more often than once per year will cause the entire account to be taxed to the owner, who will also incur the 10% penalty for failing to adhere to the rules of the College Savings Plan.

2. *Change of Account in the Same Program.* You can change accounts within the same Plan Manager's plan provided the beneficiary is *not* the same beneficiary for whom the plan was originally established. For this change to be considered tax-free, the "member of the family" rules must be followed. (see page 47.)

3. *Change to a Different Program.* You can change to a different Plan Manager's plan provided the beneficiary is *not* the same beneficiary for whom the plan was originally established. For this change to be considered tax-free, the "member of the family" rules must be followed. (see page 47.)

◆COLLEGE SAVINGS PLANS AND FINANCIAL AID

The assets in a College Savings Account are considered assets available to the family when deciding eligibility for federal financial aid. Based on available information, it appears that the money will be considered an asset of the person who owns the account. For this reason, if a parent is the owner of the account for the benefit of a child, and the child applies for financial aid, the account value will be reflected on the schedules as an asset available to the family.

Perhaps this leads to a planning opportunity. An approach that might be taken is to have the College Savings Account owned by someone other than a parent—perhaps an aunt, uncle, or grandparent. In such a case, the College Savings Account would not be included in the family's financial aid picture as the parents and children do not own the account. Of course, such a strategy has many pitfalls, including the risk that the owner dies, the owner files for bankruptcy or divorce, or the owner changes the beneficiary to be someone other than the child for whom it was originally intended. Nonetheless, under certain family circumstances, this may well work.

Chapter 4

At a Glance

THE BASICS

✦ College Savings Plans allow for the creation of a college savings account with the creator of the account typically acting as owner.

✦ The owner will retain the power to name a beneficiary of the account.

CHANGING THE BENEFICIARY

✦ The owner of the account can change the beneficiary at any time.

✦ For change of beneficiaries to be tax free, certain "family member" rules must be followed.

MAXIMUM CONTRIBUTION LIMITS AND CHANGES TO EXISTING PLANS

✦ Accounts can be changed from one Plan Manager to another on a tax free basis, provided that the change occurs only once per year.

FINANCIAL AID

✦ College Savings Plans will be considered assets of the account owner.

✦ The plan's money will be included on any financial aid form for a family where a member of the family, whether a parent or child, acts as owner of the College Savings Plan.

OWNERSHIP OF A 529 PLAN

Each 529 College Savings Plan must have an *owner* designated for the account. The owner will be the person who has control over decisions such as who the beneficiary will be, when the money will be withdrawn and for whom, and how the investments of the College Savings Plan will be maintained. Often this will be the person who opens the account. For varying reasons, including financial aid and estate planning concerns, ownership of a College Savings Plan may be in the hands of a trust, a grandparent, or other family member. When establishing the College Savings Plan account, the Plan Manager will have the owner designated on the account opening form.

Lifetime Issues

While it is clear that the owner can change the beneficiary at any time (hopefully as a tax-free change to a *member of the family*), changing ownership does not appear to be as easy. Most plans are silent on the issue, but it is reasonable to assume that changing ownership is problematic. What is clear is that the transfer of ownership, if possible under a particular state's plan, will incur a federal (and possibly a state) gift tax.

Transfer at Death

Each Plan Manager will establish their own detailed rules as to what steps are taken should the account owner die. However, generally you can expect the following.

✦Successor Owner Named

In most cases when an account is opened, the forms provided by the Plan Manager will allow an account owner to list a *successor owner* (next owner) in the event the original owner should pass away. It is important that these forms be properly completed to prevent unintended consequences if the account owner passes away. It is important to be certain that the forms that were completed when the account was opened are periodically reviewed. Be certain that there is a proper beneficiary named and there is a successor owner named in the event the owner should pass away.

✦No Successor Owner Named

When an owner of a College Savings Account dies without having named a successor owner, many Plan Manager participation agreements look to the *probate* or *surrogate* law of the state in which the owner lived. (This is the state law that controls what happens to assets when someone passes away.) In essence, the owner's last will and testament will dictate who is to become the new owner of the account. This may prove to be a serious issue as many states have probate laws that divide assets into equal or unequal shares for various beneficiaries.

Some states may provide that upon someone's death (assuming they died without a will), the spouse is to inherit one half of the assets (which would include the College Savings Plan asset), and the children are to inherit the other one-half. In such a case the College Savings Plan account may actually have 2, 3, or more owners.

> For example:
> Nicole established a College Savings Account for the benefit of her son, and Nicole is named as the owner of the account. Several years later, Nicole dies. She does not have a will and is survived by her husband and two children. Under the laws of the state in which Nicole resided, a person who dies without having a will has there assets divided so that one half goes to the spouse, with the balance being equally divided between the children. The result is that the College Savings Account will be owned one-half by her husband, and one-quarter by each of the two children. ■

To prevent this issue, each College Savings Account should have an up-to-date successor owner named in the Plan Manager's files.

TRUSTS AS OWNERS

For hundreds of years, trusts, whether revocable or irrevocable, have served as owners of assets as a means to perpetuate control over the assets. Some families may wish to consider the use of a trust as the owner, or as successor owner of a College Savings Account to be certain there is continuity of control over the assets in the College Savings Account. This may be particularly helpful in the context of establishing a College Savings Account for the benefit of grandchildren or even great-grandchildren.

Furthermore, using a trust instrument as a successor owner may allow the account owner greater control over the eventual destiny of the College Savings Plan assets than he or she might otherwise have had.

Chapter 5

At a Glance

OWNERSHIP OF A 529 PLAN

✦ Each College Savings Plan must have an owner.

✦ Typically the person opening the Account is named as the owner.

✦ The owner retains control over who the beneficiary is and who it will be.

✦ The owner has control over when assets will be withdrawn from the account and what they will be used for.

TRANSFERS AT DEATH

✦ At the death of the owner, ownership transfers to the successor owner named in the College Savings Plan documents.

✦ Ownership passes under the owner's will or state intestacy law.

TRUSTS AS OWNERS

✦ Trusts can be named as the owner of a College Savings Account to afford continuity of ownership for longer periods of time. (This may be especially appropriate in circumstances where College Savings Accounts are established for grandchildren and great-grandchildren.)

THE ROLE OF THE ADVISOR

As they now exist, College Savings Plans come in two basic types. There are plans that you can obtain without advice (what we will call "retail plans"), and plans that you obtain through an advisor ("advisor plans"). An example of a retail plan is Fidelity Retail, or the plans offered by the Teachers Insurance Annuity Association (known as TIAA/CREF). An Advisor Plan would be a plan such as Merrill Lynch's Next Gen Plan or the Fidelity Advisor Plan. Your only choice then is to purchase a College Savings Plan directly from the Plan Manager (the retail plan) or purchase the plan from an advisor (the advisor plan).

The key difference between the two plans is the advice component that the advisor plans have. How important is advice? Reasonable people may differ, but in this era, it seems to be wise to have a professional financial advisor sitting at the table when important financial decisions are made.

ISSUES FOR THE ADVISOR

While the College Savings Plan mandates that the consumer not have direct control over the investment of plan assets, the consumer still has substantial input into exactly how the savings plan will work. While fees may be involved, an advisor might be best-suited to assist the consumer with the following issues:

1. *Tax Issues.* Each College Savings Plan, as administered by the state of creation, has its own rules about state tax deductibility of investments and state taxation of distributions. An advisor should be in a position to analyze the various state tax issues and quantify any possible state tax benefits available.

2. *Investment Issues.* Plan Managers have responded to the consumer's request for greater investment options and have developed many different investment options for the assets in a College Savings Plan. Day after day Plan Managers add new offerings within their College Savings Plans. In many cases available

investment options are provided by many of the traditional investment and mutual fund companies well-known across America. A state-by-state summary of plans, and available fund managers within the plans is provided in Appendix B.

The consumer is now faced with many investment decisions within the College Savings Plan of their choice. The following is a sample of available investment options:

- age-based portfolio;
- balanced portfolio;
- growth;
- aggressive growth;
- US Large Capitalization equity growth;
- US Small Capitalization equity growth;
- US Blended Capitalization;
- high yield bond fund;
- capital preservation;
- international equity—large and small capitalization; and,
- investment grade bond funds.

The professional investment advisor is well-suited to assist a family in selecting the best investment strategy for the College Savings Plan.

The professional advisor may also be called upon to analyze for an investor the new fund offerings being brought to market on almost a daily basis by Plan Managers. As the Plan Managers compete for available 529 Plan investors, one approach will be for Plan Managers to differentiate themselves by the quantity (and hopefully quality) of the investment options available. The more Plan Managers there are, each with its own ten or fifteen investment choices, the more difficult it is to analyze.

3. *Performance Issues.* The College Savings Plan is new to the investment world, and for this reason, analyzing returns on investment for a particular portfolio must be viewed in the short-term. As the Plan Managers begin to gain experience and historical data, the performance of one Plan Manager's fund when compared to another Plan Manager's fund will become a key factor in determining the

most appropriate Plan Manager and investments for the particular College Savings Account. Investors will be in a position to analyze one Plan Manager's performance for a particular fund versus another. The professional advisor is perhaps best- suited for this type of analysis.

> For example:
> Sally opens a College Savings Account in the state of her residence as she will receive a $400 savings on her personal income tax return for contributions made to the plan. Sally invests the assets in the Plan Manager's age-based program for her son. While on its face this seems appropriate, perhaps a different course of action would be taken if Sally knew that the age-based program managed by her state's Plan Manager was under-performing all other Plan Managers by a substantial amount. In such a case, Sally might opt to forego the $400 in tax savings to achieve a better return from a Plan Manager who was experiencing a better investment return. ■

4. *Implementation and Monitoring of Plan.* The professional advisor is uniquely qualified to assist the investor in establishing the College Savings Plan and monitoring the plan over time. The following are a number of issues that require constant monitoring in a College Savings Plan, for which the professional advisor can assist:
   - proper ownership of the plan;
   - successor ownership should the plan owner die;
   - beneficiary planning, including the changing of beneficiaries;
   - plan performance and investment return; and,
   - monitoring changes in the plan itself—i.e. increase in funding limits and expansion of investment options

5. *Legislative Changes.* Plan Managers are changing their plans and states are changing the rules governing the plans on a daily basis. States are expanding the number of vendors who may act as Plan Managers and Congress continues to change and add to existing Section 529 statutes. It is important that the investor have access to the latest information about plan changes and legislative changes that affect the plan.

───────────────

■ *The example is provided for informational purposes only and does not reflect the actual* **59**
performance of any investment. All programs involve investment risk, including the loss of
principle. State taxes may be applicable.

ROLE OF THE ADVISOR IN CORPORATE-SPONSORED PLANS

Corporate-sponsored College Savings Plans will become a valuable voluntary corporate benefit offered to employees. This topic is fully discussed in Chapter 9. What will develop out of the expansion of voluntary benefit plans to include the Corporate College Savings Plan is the need for an Advisor to assist the Human Resource department in implementing the College Savings Plan. The Advisor will be in a position to determine the state plan and the Plan Managers most appropriate for the corporate program. The Advisor will also serve a key role in educating the employees about the plan and the opportunities afforded by the plan.

What may be the most important part of the advisor's services in this context is that of a *fiduciary shield* (a protector). The law provides that if a corporation that sponsors a College Savings Plan has hired a qualified financial advisor, then the corporation may be protected from possible lawsuits. An employer should be concerned that the selection of one financial services corporation, or one Plan Manager to provide the plan may expose the corporation to liability. This occurs when an employee feels that they did not get fair opportunity because of the particular Plan Manager selected. This might happen when an employee resides in a state where there is a favorable benefit for utilizing the state's home plan.

If the employer selects a plan sponsored by a different state, then the employee might feel that they did not get fair opportunity. By hiring a qualified financial advisor to help select the Plan Manager, the corporation is put in a position of taking reasonable steps to be certain that all issues an employee might encounter have been fairly considered.

As the College Savings Plans develop more widespread appeal, there will be an ever-increasing series of investment choices, state taxation considerations, internal fund costs issues, and advisor- related costs decisions that will make the selection of the appropriate College Savings Plan a challenging one. The professional financial advisor is a natural to assist in the selection of the appropriate College Savings Plan.

Chapter 6

At a Glance

ROLE OF ADVISOR

✦ College Savings Plans can be acquired in two ways: either directly (a retail plan) or through a financial advisor (an advisor plan).

ADVISOR ISSUES

✦ Issues when considering a College Savings Plan worthy of discussion with a financial advisor might be:
  • tax issues;
  • investment issues; and,
  • fund performance issues.

✦ An advisor can assist in implementing and monitoring the plan. (The various College Savings Plans have continuously added new investment options and have made changes to the underlying plan rules. An advisor will be in a position to monitor these changes and possible opportunities in other states plans.)

✦ An advisor can assist with maintaining proper ownership and successor ownership documentation as well as consulting on beneficiary planning.

✦ The advisor will be in a position to monitor law changes in this area to alert consumers to any possible positive or negative change in the governing tax laws.

ADVISOR'S ROLE IN CORPORATE-SPONSORED PLANS

✦ In the context of the Corporate Provided College Savings 529 plan, the advisor can assist with the selection of the primary Plan Manager as well as assist with the education and implementation for employees.

ESTATE PLANNING AND
THE COLLEGE SAVINGS PLAN

Much of our focus has been on the opportunity the College Savings Plan provides in the context of saving for college. Not quite as obvious is the estate planning opportunity to be achieved by using the College Savings Plan as a wealth transfer vehicle.

FEDERAL ESTATE PLANNING BASICS

The College Savings Plan is a federal program administered by each state in a slightly different manner. Since each state will have a different way of dealing with gift and estate taxes, our discussion here focuses solely on the federal estate tax and gift tax systems. As with the income tax difference from state to state that make the selection of an appropriate College Savings Account a complicated task, so must state gift and estate taxes be considered.

Under the current federal system governing gifts and estate taxes, each person is allowed to make gifts each year to as many people (related or not) as they like in an amount of $11,000 to each—free of any gift tax. Married couples can join together to double this per person gift to be an annual $22,000. In addition to these gifts, each person has a lifetime $1,000,000 exemption amount for gifts above this annual limit. To the extent the lifetime exemption amount is not used, then the remaining balance can be used at death to offset any estate taxes. This exemption amount is scheduled to increase substantially over the next several years.

For example:
Nicole has three children, each of whom she would like to make a gift to this year (2002). Nicole writes a check to each child in the amount

of $11,000. This gift qualifies under the allowable gift tax annual exclusion, and so the gift is a non-taxable gift that does not require the filing of a gift tax return. ■

Mary and Allen have three children, each of whom they would like to make a gift to this year (2002). Mary writes a check to each child in the amount of $22,000. This gift qualifies under the allowable gift tax annual exclusion, and so the gift is a non-taxable gift. In this case since Mary and Allen are joining together to treat the gifts as being half from each person (*gift-splitting*), Mary and Allen need to file a gift tax return to document the gift-splitting. There is still no gift tax to be paid. ■

Sally has three children, each of whom she would like to make a gift to this year (2002). Sally writes a check to each child in the amount of $111,000. This gift qualifies under the allowable gift tax annual exclusion, and so the first $11,000 of each gift is a non-taxable gift. The additional $100,000 per child amount in excess of the $11,000 reduces Sally's lifetime exemption amount from the original $1,000,000 by the amount of these gifts, ($300,000). Sally must file a gift tax return to report that she has used up a portion of her lifetime exemption amount. There is still no gift tax to be paid. ■

College Savings Plans— Estate Planning Rules

◆ Gift Rules

In an effort to help families begin the savings process, the Section 529 rules allow for the *front-end loading* of a College Savings Account. This means that the rules allow for more than the annual $11,000 per person gift. The rules allow for 5 times that amount. (It is recognized as $11,000 each year over 5 years that are allowed by the rules.) So a single person can transfer $55,000 to a College Savings Account for a person and not have any amount of the gift reduce their lifetime credit amount. Married couples can join together to make this a $110,000 gift without any amount reducing their lifetime credits. By setting up the gift-giving rules this way, the tax-deferred savings is a more meaningful ability.

The rules even allow you to stay up-to-date with current gift-giving law. The rules provide that if the amount of the annual exclusion increases and you have already made a gift that you are "stretching" over the five year allowable period, then you are allowed to add to the account in an amount designed to let you use the full annual gift exclusion amount.

> For example:
>
> In 2000 (when $10,000 was the maximum tax-free gift allowed), Mary made a gift of $50,000 to her daughter and had the money invested in a College Savings Account. Mary made the necessary election to have the amounts spread evenly over five years, so that the gift is treated as the allowable $10,000 per year. In 2002, the tax law changes and the annual exclusion amount increases to $11,000 per year per person. Mary is allowed to add to the College Savings Account the increase of $1,000 per year for each of the remaining years the original gift is being spread over. In this case, there would be three remaining years on the original five year even spread of the gift (2002, 2003 and 2004 remain) and so Mary may add an amount up to the $3,000 additional amount.

There is a bit of a catch when making these larger up-front gifts. If you make a gift that is more than the annual amount (currently $11,000), then the rules give you the option of treating the excess as being used up equally over a five year period as though you annually made the $11,000 gift, or use up some of your lifetime $1,000,000 exemption amount. Since most people attempt to save the exemption amount, or certainly use the "free" annual exclusion amount first, it will be common for people to use the ability to "spread" the gifts over five years. If you do this, and you pass away during this 5-year period, part of the original gift (not the growth) will be brought back into your estate for tax purposes.

> For example:
>
> In 2002 Mary makes a gift of $55,000 to her daughter and has the money invested in a College Savings Account. Mary makes the necessary election to have the amounts in excess of the annual $11,000 amount

(here an excess of $44,000) spread evenly over the remaining four years (five years less the first year's $11,000 exclusion amount). Mary dies in 2004 when the College Savings Account value is $75,000.

Mary's estate must include the portion of the original gift that has not been fully covered by the five annual exclusions. In this case, Mary will have used three exclusions (2002, 2003 and 2004 at $11,000 each year) and will have two remaining years of exclusions that have not been used. For this reason Mary's estate (for tax purposes) must include the $22,000 (2005 and 2006 at $11,000 each year) of gifts which were not covered by the exclusion. Even though $22,000 worth of the gift is being included in Mary's taxable estate, the growth that has been achieved on this money does not get included in her taxable estate. ■

✦CONTROL

One of the more amazing things about the College Savings Plan, and the related gift planning, is that this may be the first gift ever to be created where the person giving the gift can redirect who will get the gift. Under traditional gift tax rules, if a person made a gift, but kept some element of control over both the gift and who the eventual beneficiary would be (or just had the power to change beneficiaries even if the power was never exercised), the gift was treated as an incomplete gift. This means that the full amount of the original gift and any *appreciation* on the gift would not be treated as a gift for gift tax purposes. When the person who made the original gift, but kept control, eventually died, he or she would be taxed in full for the value of the gift.

The 529 Plan rules specifically allow for the owner of the account (most often the person who puts the money into the account) to maintain control over the account—even control over who will receive it and when. The rules specifically state that retaining this control will not cause the amount in the account to be taxed to the owner at his or her death. Finally, people can make gifts, but feel as though they did not give up that single most important of items—control.

For example:
Sally makes a gift of $11,000 to her daughter, Alexia, and places the money in a *joint account* with Alexia. Sally continues to retain control (she can take money out of the joint account anytime she wishes).

Should Sally pass away, the full amount of the account at the time of her death will be included in her taxable estate. ■

Nicole makes a gift of $11,000 and places the money in a College Savings Account. Nicole names her daughter, Ellen, as the beneficiary. Ten years later, when the account has grown to be $60,000, Nicole takes Ellen's name off the account and places Steven's name on the account. Even though Nicole has made a gift, but kept control over who will have the beneficial enjoyment, at Nicole's death no amount of the gift will be included in her taxable estate for estate tax purposes. ■

Even beyond the ability to change the beneficiary, the owner of the account has the ability to close the account and take back all of the money at anytime. Of course doing so will subject the assets to the ordinary income tax on all of the gains, and the penalty tax of 10%, but perhaps in some cases this may seem a small price to pay to be certain the "right" thing happens.

CREATIVE ESTATE PLANNING

Never before have estate planners had such a powerful gift-giving tool to add to their arsenal of gift-giving strategies. The ability to grow assets tax-deferred, while continuing to maintain complete control over who is the beneficiary, affords families with estate tax exposure a new way to plan away these estate taxes.

For a family that has a substantial net worth that will cause them to face an estate tax, the funding of a College Savings Account is not just to save for college. It is also an opportunity to save for college for grandchildren and great-grandchildren even those not yet born. Since the College Savings Account allows for the changing of beneficiary, tax-free at any time (as long as the *member of the family* rules on page 47 are followed), the opportunity exists to begin shifting assets to a lower generation without really knowing who will eventually benefit from the gift. By using the College Savings Plan as a gift-giving tool, it is now possible to make gifts, and begin the shifting of all growth on those gifts, without using any lifetime gift tax exemption amount, and never losing control. (We recommend the reader consult an attorney for specific estate planning assistance.)

For example:

Mary makes a gift of $11,000 into a College Savings Account and names herself as beneficiary. Mary does this each year for a series of five years. Twenty years later, when the account has grown to a value of $200,000, Mary takes her name off the account and names her fifteen year-old grandson as the beneficiary. Mary has accomplished a tax-free gift, generation skipping tax-free, and a tax-free estate transfer of a substantial amount by using the College Savings Account as the investment vehicle. During all of the years prior to naming her grandson, and the years after naming him, Mary has maintained complete control over the account, including when it would be used and for whom. ■

The "Double Dip" Opportunity

Current gift-giving rules allow for the payment of tuition expenses without having to use any of your annual gift-giving exclusion amounts or the lifetime exemption amount. For this reason, grandparents are often advised to write a check directly to pay tuition at a school their grandchild attends rather than making the gift to the grandchild to use for tuition. In fact, there are cases where older individuals are encouraged to pre-pay all four years of college tuition for their grandchildren in an effort to use as much of their assets as possible. That way those assets will not be included in their taxable estates. When someone is older and may not survive all four years of college tuition-paying, the prepayment option makes sense.

In the context of the College Savings Account this type of planning continues to make sense. If a grandparent is in a position to pay the tuition directly to the college or university, then the grandparent should do so. In so doing the amounts transferred to the school will escape all forms of gift tax and estate tax under existing law. Once the tuition has been paid, the grandparent can then add additional gift funds to a College Savings Account to be used to pay room, board, books, supplies, etc.

For example:

Sally writes a check to Yale University for her granddaughter's college tuition of $30,000. In addition, Sally makes a gift of $11,000 to her granddaughter and places the money in a College Savings Account. The money in the College Savings Account is then used to pay for books, supplies, equipment, etc. ■

THE UNINTENDED GIFT TAX CONSEQUENCE

As we have explored at length, the owner of the College Savings Account can change the beneficiary at anytime as long as the "member of the family" sets of rules are followed. Be careful though. When a change of beneficiary moves the beneficiary to someone a generation lower than the original beneficiary, then a gift has been made. In this case, the gift is treated as being made by the beneficiary to the new beneficiary. If the new beneficiary is more than one generation below the original beneficiary, then not only is it a gift, but it may also be a generation-skipping gift and may subject the assets to the generation-skipping tax.

> For example:
> In 2000, Nicole made a gift of $55,000 to her daughter, Ellen, and had the money invested in a College Savings Account. Fifteen years later, when the account value has grown to $150,000, Nicole removes her daughter's name and places her granddaughter's name on the College Savings Account. In this case, the naming of the granddaughter is treated as a gift from Ellen to the granddaughter of the entire amount value of the College Savings Account. Ellen would use her annual gift tax exclusion amount as well as some amount of her lifetime credit exemption amount to prevent this gift from resulting in a gift tax. ■

OWNERSHIP ISSUES AND ESTATE PLANNING

The nature of the College Savings Account is that there is an owner who controls everything, and a beneficiary who hopes that the owner uses the account assets for the beneficiary's qualified higher education expenses. What cannot be lost in this exercise is the concern that the owner of the account might die. This will leave the question of who becomes the new owner. Many of the Plan Managers have recognized this concern and have provided space on their application forms of the name of a *contingent* or *successor* owner on the account. Some applications do not contain this request for information, and even when they do request the name of a successor owner, not everyone fully completes the form. It is extremely important to have a successor owner named to be the person who will have all rights to change the beneficiary, determine when assets are drawn from the account, etc.

What happens when there is no successor owner named, or the successor owner is not living at the time of the owner's death? The answer lies in the state's property and descent laws. Simply, the College Savings Account will become an asset of the person who died (the *decedent*) and will pass either through the person's will if he or she had one. If the person passed away and did not have a will, then ownership of the account will pass to the deceased person's heirs as required by state law.

Consider the problem then, if a person who is single, who has a College Savings Account for a nephew, dies without a will. If the owner had no parents but three siblings, the state's laws might have all three siblings inherit the account. In this case, two of the siblings who do not have children might want to distribute their share of the College Savings Account, leaving only the one sibling with a child to keep the account intact.

To avoid this, be certain a contingent or successor owner is named on the College Savings Account, or that the terms of your will make a specific reference as to who will become the new owner of the College Savings Account if you were to pass away.

POST DEATH TRUST ISSUES

Of great concern is the steps that need to be taken when the owner of a College Savings Account dies leaving a will that transfers all assets to a trust. Sometimes these trusts that receive assets at death are extremely complicated and may not be an appropriate place for a College Savings Account. In fact, it is common for married couples to have special types of wills and trusts designed to utilize the federal unified credit against estate taxes. These types of trusts, known as *by-pass* trusts, mandate certain uses and distributions of principal and income. If the College Savings Account is an asset that gets swept into a by-pass trust, unfortunate results may occur. If the College Savings Account is an asset that gets swept into the by-pass trust, unintended results may occur.

If the by-pass trust is drafted in a traditional manner allowing for the use of the assets for a variety of needs, including education expenses, then the College Savings Account may continue to work as originally intended.

A further problem that may occur after death is when a College Savings Account is transferred into a marital trust. One form of a marital trust, know as a *Qualified Terminable Interest Property Trust* (QTIP) is generally for the surviving spouse only. A QTIP trust is required by tax law to generate income on the principal to the trust. This is far different from the College Savings Account which does not generally create income and if it did would not have any income distributed. The trustee of a QTIP trust might be put in a position of having to close the College Savings Account and withdraw the money as cash to properly move forward in his or her job as trustee.

In either case, if the College Savings Account was intact at the time of the spouse's death and the Account was in a QTIP trust, then the entire account balance would be included in the surviving spouse's estate under the federal estate tax rules applicable to QTIP trusts. The answer then is to be certain to properly plan for a successor or contingent owner on the College Savings Account to be certain the ownership of the account does not end up in an unfortunate trust setting.

DEATH OF A COLLEGE SAVINGS PLAN BENEFICIARY

The law provides that if a beneficiary of a College Savings Plan dies, then the full value of the College Savings Account is included in the beneficiary's estate for estate tax purposes. It would be unusual for a child for whom a College Savings Account had been established to pass away. However, there are times when an account owner will know of the possible impending death of the beneficiary. The owner would then change the beneficiary to prevent any amount from being included in the beneficiary's estate.

As noted above, in 2002 the first one million dollars of assets in an estate pass free of federal estate tax. The inclusion in a beneficiary's estate is therefore only an estate tax issue when the beneficiary has one million dollars or more of assets, plus a College Savings Account when he or she dies.

> For example:
> In 2003, Jane, a beneficiary of a 529 Account, passes away. At the time of Jane's death, she was unmarried and had total assets of $1,400,000. In addition, Jane was the beneficiary of a College Savings Account that had $200,000. The combined amount of $1,600,000 is more than the existing estate tax-free credit of $1,000,000. For this reason, Jane's estate will pay estate tax on the amount greater than $1,000,000 ($600,000).

STRANGE POSSIBILITIES

Congress will need to continually update and modify the Section 529 rules. As presently drafted, unintended results may occur from time to time.

Consider the circumstance where a father makes annual gifts to his children's several College Savings Accounts in annual amounts of $44,000 ($11,000 for each of his 4 children). The father dies and provides for no successor owner in the Plan Managers records. In such a case the father's will takes control, and if the father's will leaves everything to his wife, she becomes the new owner of the accounts.

Under the estate tax rules, nothing is included in the father's estate as these were completed gifts utilizing the father's annual exclusions. Even though the father utilized his annual gift tax exclusion, the ownership of the account passes to his wife not to the beneficiaries. The wife could now close the 529 accounts and take back all the money in the accounts.

To prevent any problems, it is important to have an updated set of ownership forms on these documents. In addition, it may make sense to begin having wills specifically state that a College Savings Plan owned by a person who passes away is to pass to a specific individual who will be the new owner of the account.

What happens if one of the children for whom an account was established were to pass away? Under the general rules, the child would include in his her own estate the full amount of the account. This full inclusion occurs even though the mother continues to maintain complete control over the account and can name a new beneficiary or even distribute the account for herself. It is strange that the beneficiary is subjected to estate taxation on assets in an account that he or she did not have control of, and might never have benefited from if the mother or father had changed the beneficiary to be someone else.

Chapter 7

At a Glance

College Savings Plans and Estate Planning Rules

✦ Annual gifts up to the annual gift tax free amount of $11,000 per person can be deposited into a College Savings Plan account and qualify as a gift tax free transfer.

✦ Married couples can join together to make this a $22,000 per year gift.

✦ *Front-end loading* of a College Savings Plan account is allowed where five times the annual gift tax amount ($11,000) can be made at one time.

✦ Gifts can be made by grandparents to grandchildren utilizing the annual gift tax exclusion and annual generation skipping tax exclusion, both in the amount of $11,000 per person per year.

Creative Estate Planning

✦ Gift strategies might include the *double dip* opportunity where tuition is paid directly to an institution by a family member (these payments do not count against the annual gift tax exclusion) and additional funds are deposited into a College Savings Plan account for the benefit of the child attending the college.

Unintended Gift Tax

✦ Changes in beneficiaries on a College Savings Account can cause the account to be taxed as either a gift or generation skipping transfer or both. (This occurs when a beneficiary change is made to the account and the beneficiary is in a generation lower than the original beneficiary was.)

(continued)

Ownership Issues and Estate Planning

✦ Ownership of a 529 College Savings Plan is an asset that will pass through a deceased person's estate.

✦ A successor owner needs to be named on the account forms maintained by the Plan Manager to be certain that thee is a successor owner in the event the owner passes away.

Post Death Trust Issues

✦ Unintended results can occur when College Savings Account is transferred into a trust at the death of the account owner.

✦ Particular problems may occur when the trust into which the College Savings Account is transferred is a martial trust or a Qualified Terminable Interest Property (QTIP) type of marital trust.

Death of A Beneficiary

✦ Amounts may be included in a beneficiary's taxable estate for federal estate tax purposes if they were to pass away with assets in a College Savings Account.

THE "NEW" EMPLOYEE BENEFIT

Employees can now establish Section 529 College Savings Plans through their employer as a voluntary employee benefit. This chapter discusses the Section 529 Plan as an employee benefit, the advantages of establishing a plan through your employer, and the way to find out if your employer offers a 529 Plan as an employee benefit.

UNDERSTANDING EMPLOYEE BENEFIT PLANS

For years companies have enabled employees to purchase benefits for themselves and their families through employer-sponsored plans. These benefits can include insurance products, as well as financial products. Many have medical insurance, dental insurance, life insurance and retirement savings plans through such employer-sponsored plans. In such a case the employer has established these plans for the benefit of the employees. The employer maintains and administers the benefit plans, providing a simple and effective means for the employee to obtain these important programs—very often at great savings to the employees.

Purchasing benefits through an employer has also become convenient for the employee over the years. Access to insurance and financial products is part of the convenience. In addition, many employers allow individuals to pay for their benefits through payroll deduction. The payroll deduction feature is an important advantage of the employer-sponsored plan. Allowing an employer to deduct premiums or account deposits directly from a paycheck eliminates the need for the employee to write the checks necessary to maintain these products. Payroll deduction benefits enable an employee to budget for these benefits. The advantages available through payroll deduction are rarely found in the individual marketplace without an added cost.

Finally, employee benefit plans allow individuals to take advantage of the power of group purchasing. Group purchasing often results in more cost effective pricing (i.e., lower cost to the participant), enhanced access to a wide range of programs, fewer restrictions on participation, and enhanced benefit options. In many cases the group purchased program is more advantageous to the consumer than the individual program.

EXPANDING BENEFIT PLANS

Over the years, companies have recognized the value that employees place on the benefits available to them through their place of employment and have begun to expand the benefit choices available to their workforce. Some employers are taking an active role in helping their employees balance their work and life needs. Offering additional benefits plans to their employees is one way that some companies are helping employees achieve this balance. It makes sense and can achieve positive outcomes for both employee and employer.

Employee benefit plans are used by many employers as an effective tool in recruiting quality employees, and retaining a loyal employee workforce. At the same time, companies recognize that their individual employees have diverse needs. The new employee benefits program often includes numerous voluntary financial and insurance plans that meet the needs of a diverse workforce. In fact, what some might consider nontraditional benefit plans, are frequently offered by large corporate employers. These nontraditional benefits are typically voluntary in nature (paid for in full by the individual participants). In addition to other offerings, these benefits may include such programs as automobile insurance, disability insurance, life insurance, long term care insurance, and legal advice plans, to name a few.

This means that individuals are gaining access to a whole host of new benefit programs, programs that are valuable and important to them. One great thing about these voluntary benefit plans is that each individual participant can pick and choose which parts of the plans are important to them and within their budget constraints.

Keep in mind that not all companies offer such comprehensive benefit plans. Smaller companies for example may provide limited or no benefits for their employees. In some situations, smaller companies just do not have the staff to administer such programs. However, it is important to know that many companies with as few as 50–100 employees offer benefits, often with some voluntary plans.

ADDING 529 PLANS TO THE PACKAGE

The Section 529 College Savings Plan joins the benefits package as one of the newest nontraditional employee benefits to be offered by employers. Companies recognize that saving for college is an important goal for many families. Recent changes in federal tax laws make 529 Plans an advantageous way for many individuals to reach their college savings goal for their family. Finally, companies recognize that by offering a 529 Plan they can improve employee feelings about the company, and thus, employee loyalty.

✦ADVANTAGES OF THE EMPLOYER-SPONSORED 529 PLAN

In many ways, an employer-sponsored 529 Plan is similar to benefit plans discussed earlier. It has many of the advantages of an employer-sponsored medical plan, for example.

An employer-sponsored 529 College Savings Plan can offer a simple solution to a college savings program that can often be quite complex. Consider the issues. Each state has its own state-sponsored 529 Plan, which may be administered by one or more Plan Managers. Each of these state plans and Plan Managers has its own design features, tax issues, and investment choices. It can be overwhelming to think that each and every 529 College Savings Plan participant could research all of the available plans to be able to select the one plan that best meets their needs.

The employer-sponsored 529 Plan can alleviate some of this complexity from the selection and enrollment process, and in many cases offer a program that is equivalent to or better than an individually acquired College Savings Plan. This is not to suggest that individuals should enroll in an employer-sponsored plan without researching the options available to them. Each individual's situation and goals are different and should be treated as such. Nonetheless, an employer-sponsored plan can be implemented by a corporation, with the goal of providing a valuable benefit to employees.

In addition to simplifying the process of selecting a Plan Manager and enrolling, the employer-sponsored 529 Plan offers convenient and flexible contribution arrangements. Like many traditional employee benefit plans, employer-sponsored 529 Plans can offer the convenience of payroll deduction or direct deposit. This feature allows individuals to invest an amount they can afford through an easy, automatic, and consistent vehicle. In many cases, minimum deposits in the 529 Plan are lower through an employer-sponsored plan than through an individual plan. At the same time, maximum allowable contributions are often higher through the employer-sponsored plan than they are under an individual plan. Each element is negotiated as part of a contract on behalf of a group of employees rather than a single individual.

Another benefit of group purchasing is the advantage of lower expenses to the fund manager. Individuals participating in a College Savings 529 Plan pay sales fees or loads to acquire the College Savings Plan. Often, these expense loads are reduced for group program offerings. These negotiated reductions are the result of economies of scale available when programs are offered to large groups of individuals. Lower expenses result in more money in the College Savings Account.

Further, in some situations individuals can benefit from expanded investment options for their savings dollars. While some state plans may limit the investment funds from which participants can choose, the employer-sponsored plans are normally with Plan Managers that offer the 529 College Savings Plan through advisors. They often provide additional investment options to meet the needs of a diverse workforce. Additional investment options allow each individual participant to invest their college savings as aggressively or conservatively as they choose within the fund options available. Once again, this advantage results from negotiations undertaken by the employer on behalf of its group of employees.

Finally, it is important to highlight one additional advantage of the corporate-provided College Savings Plan. The benefit is in the availability of a professional advisor. The role of the investment advisor is to explain the various options available to individual participants and advise them in selecting the investment strategy and fund selection for their particular circumstance. The advisor is available to help individuals sort through the various state plans relative to the group plan offering and also to provide advice to those participants who may be better served through another college savings vehicle.

The investment advisor may be a valuable resource to individuals, but traditionally the consumer must select and pay for the advisor on their own. Given the complex nature of saving for college and the expected changes states will continue to make to their College Savings Plans, the investment advisor is a very important feature for those group 529 Plans that provide for investment counseling.

✦ EMPLOYER-SPONSORED VERSUS STATE-SPONSORED PLANS

It is important to understand that employer-sponsored 529 Plans have been developed to offer some of the most comprehensive features and advantages that are available through the various state plans. In addition, some employer-sponsored plans offer advantages not available through the individual state plans, for example payroll deduction. Therefore, in many cases the employer-sponsored plan will be the best choice for individuals wherever possible.

Nonetheless, in some situations a state sponsored program not provided by an employer may be more advantageous to an individual. Such a situation could occur if an individual resides in a state where the state plan allows for plan contributions to be deducted on state income tax returns. The state tax deduction may or may not be advantageous to the individual participant considering an employer-sponsored plan.

Because each individual's situation is unique and each individual has his or her own objectives and priorities, it is important to consider the many options available for college savings. If your employer's plan has made an investment advisor available to the individual plan participants, discuss your personal situation with the advisor. He or she will be able to help you sort through your options.

DETERMINING IF YOUR EMPLOYER OFFERS A 529 PLAN

If you work for a large company, your employer is more likely to offer nontraditional voluntary benefit plans. Larger companies tend to offer the greatest number of voluntary benefits. Large companies often have diverse workforces with diverse benefit needs. In addition, large companies sometimes have more support in the administration of these plans. That is not to say that some mid to small sized companies do not offer very comprehensive benefit plans with numerous employee benefit options. Many do. And many will likely consider adding a Section 529 Plan to their benefit program.

How do you find out if your employer offers a 529 Plan? The best way is to ask. Your company's human resource department is a good place to start. They are typically involved in the benefits administration and will be able to advise you if your company has a plan. They should also be able to provide you with information about your company's plan or direct you to the person or place with the information you need.

If your employer tells you that they do not offer a College Savings 529 Plan, ask if they are considering adding the benefit in the future. Your company may be researching the various 529 options or in the process of implementing a plan to be rolled-out to employees later in the year. If it is a benefit that is important to you, let them know that you would value an employer-sponsored 529 Plan. Perhaps others have indicated a similar interest.

In general, companies want to provide benefit plans that will get individual participation and will be valued. Companies often have to make choices about what plans they will offer. Your input could be important.

Given employee support of voluntary benefits, the recent federal tax changes, and the importance individuals place on saving for college, many in the employee benefits field anticipate that the employer-sponsored 529 Plan will be among the benefit choices offered in many companies.

A Word of Caution

While it is true that most employer offerings on a group basis have built into them some savings achieved by the large group purchase, it does not always mean that the group product is appropriate. Since there are many College Savings Plans available, and the decision of which plan to purchase is a function of many factors, it is important that the consumer determine which College Savings Plan is appropriate. Discussions with an expert or advisor, a side-by-side comparison of the individually purchased product and the group product, the comparison of expenses, tax deductions, etc. all factor into the decision of whether the corporate-sponsored 529 Plan is the appropriate plan for the particular employee. There is no solution for saving for college that fits all individual circumstances.

Chapter 8

At a Glance

CORPORATE-SPONSORED PLANS

✦ College Savings Plans can be obtained through the corporate workplace as a voluntary employee benefit.

✦ When utilizing a corporate-provided College Savings Plan the employee is afforded access to the same College Savings Plans as exist in the marketplace.

EMPLOYEE BENEFIT PLANS

✦ Corporate-provided plans provide access to the employees at a reduced cost.

✦ Properly designed corporate-provided College Savings Plans will have an advisor involved in the program for purpose of advising and implementing the plan.

✦ Corporate-provided College Savings Plans will afford greater access to greater numbers of people and in many cases will enhance the likelihood of success in saving for college by offering payroll deducted contributions.

SCHOLARSHIP PROGRAMS AND THE 529 PLAN

Section 529, in addition to creating a tax-favored means for families to save for college, provides a new way for charities to fund education-related scholarship programs. The controlling language that creates this opportunity is not particularly clear since scholarship programs are a part of the larger discussion focusing on permissible beneficiaries.

In part, Section 529(e)(1)(C) defines a *designated beneficiary* of a College Savings Account, as "the individual receiving a distribution for qualified higher education expenses as part of a scholarship program maintained by a 501(C)(3) charity". This means that if a scholarship program maintained by a charity establishes a College Savings Plan for the investments of the charitable funds, then any distribution to a person for qualified higher education expenses will qualify as a permissible beneficiary of a College Savings Account.

TRADITIONAL CHARITIES AND COLLEGE SAVINGS PLANS

The application of the College Savings Plan to traditional charities is limited in nature. Since charities (assuming qualified under Internal Revenue Code, Section 501(C)(3)) do not pay income or capital gains taxes, the use of the College Savings Plan to invest assets on a tax-deferred basis is limited. This will, however, allow the assets that are specifically designed for scholarship funds to be separately maintained on the books of the charity. The charity will be able to use the institutional expertise of the Plan Managers to help grow these scholarship funds.

The College Savings Account maintained by a charity would be an aggregate account holding all scholarship funds. When a scholarship grant is awarded, the College Savings Account maintained by the charity will have the beneficiary designation revised to name the person receiving the scholarship.

ESTABLISHING THE SCHOLARSHIP PROGRAM

Section 529 allows any state or local government, or traditional charity (501(c)(3) qualified) to establish a scholarship program utilizing the benefits of the College Savings Plan. These charitable organizations are typically designed to promote charitable, scientific, literary, educational, and religious pursuits. The charity would establish, in most cases, a single College Savings Plan into which all contributions for the scholarship are deposited. The charity would name itself as the beneficiary of the College Savings Account, waiting for the designation of a person as the recipient of the scholarship. Once the scholarship is awarded, the College Savings Account would be changed to reflect that the recipient would be the new beneficiary of a portion of the account.

The law allows for the change of a beneficiary on a *charity's* College Savings Account without any reference to the family members of the prior beneficiary. (see page 83.) The scholarship program can change beneficiaries at any time without any negative tax consequence.

Even though there appears to be greater flexibility when a charity establishes a College Savings Account for funding scholarships, the rules relating to maximum contribution limits remain. For this reason the charity can only fund the College Savings Account to the maximum limit established by the state's laws.

A positive difference between charitable College Savings Accounts and these same accounts maintained by individuals relates to the *re-filling* of the account once a scholarship has been made. With the traditional individual College Savings Account, once the maximum contribution limit has been reached for a particular beneficiary, no further funding may take place. That is, even after one year of college has depleted more than was estimated for the child's expenses, leaving insufficient funds for the balance of college expenses, no further funding can be made. This prohibition of additional funding for the benefit of the same beneficiary is a state-by-state requirement to qualify for this federal program. It may be possible, but certainly ill advised to have a College Savings Account in each state for the same child and fund the accounts to the maximum per state. You may run the risk that you are deemed to be violating federal tax law. This type of activity might be considered to be tax evasion by the Internal Revenue Service.

In the charity-sponsored College Savings Account, after a scholarship has been awarded and the funds distributed, additional funds can thereafter be added to the College Savings Account to bring the Account total back up to the maximum funding limit.

For example:

Mary establishes a College Savings Account and funds the account to the maximum level allowed, which under the state's rules is a total of $200,000. When her son attends college, Mary is shocked as the actual first year's expenses will total $65,000. Mary realizes that after the first year is paid, there will be insufficient funds in the account to pay the remaining three years. Even though Mary has removed the first year's $65,000 from the account she cannot add to the account to bring it back up to the maximum contribution level. Once the maximum contribution level has been reached, no further contributions can be made. ■

For example:

Xanadu Charity establishes a College Savings Account for the purpose of investing assets set aside for scholarships to be granted to students attending college. In 2002, the account was funded to the state limit of $200,000. Xanadu Charity makes six scholarship awards in 2002, each in the amount of $10,000. After making the distributions to the scholarship recipients, Xanadu Charity can add to the account the amount needed (in this case $60,000) to bring the account back to the maximum contribution limit. ■

UNIVERSITIES AND COLLEGES— COMPENSATION PLANNING

A creative use of the College Savings Account is in the compensation arena. This is most certainly the case when the College Savings Account is coupled with colleges and universities that provide certain educational benefits to employees and their children.

It is not unusual, as an employee benefit, for colleges and universities to afford their employees some form of contribution towards the college-related expenses of an employee's children. Many colleges and universities allow children of an employee to attend the college of employment at a reduced level or in some cases free of charge. These same colleges and universities may provide an economic benefit for those children of employees who attend colleges or universities other than the one at which the parent is employed. It is in this instance that the College Savings Plan can have great impact.

Traditionally, if a child of a qualified employee (qualified based upon the rules established by the college or university) were to attend a school other than the employing school, the employee would receive the benefit from the employer in the form of additional compensation or bonus. In its simplest form, the employee would provide evidence of having paid the college expenses of the child and receive a check as reimbursement. The amount received by the employee would be taxed to the employee as compensation for ordinary income tax. It is possible that one-third or more of the benefit paid by the employer could be lost to income taxation.

By utilizing the College Savings Plan as a way to provide the employee benefit, a level of taxation can be eliminated.

For example:

Xanadu University provides a benefit to employees who have worked at the university for more than seven years. These employees may send their children (assuming they qualify for admission) to Xanadu University free of charge. If a qualifying employee has a child that does not attend Xanadu University, but attends another eligible college or university, then Xanadu will contribute $10,000 per year to assist the employee/parent with the college expenses of the child. This $10,000 is treated as compensation to the employee and must be included in his or her taxable income.

In 2002, Xanadu learned of the College Savings Plan and put in place a program to be used to fund these commitments to the children of qualifying employees. Xanadu funded the College Savings Account with enough money to fully satisfy its expenses for the year. All further payments to employees for the college expenses of the employee's children were made from the College Savings Accounts. By doing so, the distributions to the child are treated as permissible tax-free (assuming the funds are used for qualified higher education expenses) distributions from the College Savings Account and are not included in the employee's income. ■

✦The Real Difference

Prior to the College Savings Plan, when Xanadu wrote a check for the college expenses of the employee's child ordinary income tax was paid on the money as compensation. Without a College Savings Account as the means to pay this reimbursement of college expenses, if the employee were in the 25% tax bracket, then of the $10,000 grant, $2,500 would be lost to taxation. Under the College Savings Plan approach, when the $10,000 is distributed out of the plan, no portion is subjected to taxation, allowing the full $10,000 to be used by the child for higher education-related expenses.

Corporate-Sponsored College Savings Accounts— Compensation Planning

✦Voluntary Corporate Benefit

As was discussed in Chapter 7, the College Savings Plan can be a valuable voluntary employee benefit provided by an employer. Having access to a corporate-provided College Savings Plan, the employee can obtain the very same College Savings Plan administered by one of the Plan Managers as could be achieved without the corporate sponsor, but at a much lower price.

Often the cost to a non-corporate provided plan can be as much as seven times more expensive than the corporate-provided plan. This occurs when an advisor-provided College Savings Plan is purchased by a consumer at a 3.5% commission to the advisor, versus the corporate-provided plan which can be obtained for one-half of one percent (seven times less than the advisor-provided plan). If the corporate-provided plan can be obtained with the same quality advice component, and have the ability to deduct the contributions from payroll, then the employee is afforded a great advantage over non-corporate-provided plans.

✦Corporate Matching Contributions

In the 401(k) arena it is common for employers to establish a matching formula to provide a motivation to employees to save for their retirement. This also creates a loyalty bond between employer and employee which enhances the quality of the employment relationship. Since the matching contribution takes the form of additional funding of the tax favored 401(k) plan, there is no additional compensation to the employee. Rather, the corporate contributions are added to the employee's

401(k) balance and no tax is incurred until the employee begins taking withdrawals from the 401(k) sometime down the road.

The logical question then is whether an employer can make *matching* type contributions to an employee's College Savings Account to promote the virtues of saving for college and create this loyalty bond.

The College Savings Plan is not a qualified retirement plan, and does not qualify for tax deductible contributions. Any such corporate matching contribution is treated as additional compensation to the employee, and the *matching* amount is taxed.

For example:
Millie's Marvelous Meatballs annually matches all 401(k) contributions made by its employees. During the year, Sally contributed $10,000 to her 401(k). Millie's Marvelous Meatballs provides a 3% match of contributions, and deposits into Sally's 401(k) account the sum of $300. Since the additional $300 was deposited into the 401(k), Sally does not have to report any additional income and does not pay any tax on the contribution until funds are withdrawn from the 401(k). ■

For example:
Chocolate Chips, Inc. establishes a Corporate-Sponsored, voluntary College Savings Plan to assist employees with their efforts to save for college expenses. Chocolate Chips, Inc. agrees to add 3% of an employee's contributions to the College Savings Account, not to exceed $300 on an annual basis. During the year, Nicole contributed $10,000 to her College Savings Account for her son. Chocolate Chips, Inc. provides a 3% match of contributions, and deposits into the College Savings Account the sum of $300. Since the College Savings Plan is not a qualified retirement plan, the additional $300 deposited into the College Savings Account is treated as income and will be taxed to Nicole. ■

✦Corporate-Sponsored Scholarship Programs— A Possible Solution

A strategy that might be employed to allow for *matching* type contributions by an employer without causing the contributions to be taxed to the employee would be to involve the use of a corporate-created charitable scholarship fund. Since the

529 Plan rules allow for the use of a College Savings Account for purpose of maintaining a charitable scholarship fund, one approach would be to have the sponsoring corporation create a charitable foundation for the purpose of making scholarship awards to children of qualifying employees.

The Plan

Let's assume that ABC Corporation establishes a voluntary College Savings Plan for its employees. In an effort to assist its employees in their effort to save sufficient funds for college, ABC Corporation agrees to contribute a fixed sum, perhaps $300 per employee participating in the college savings plan. Since ABC Corporation understands that this type of *matching* contribution to a College Savings Plan will force the employee to treat the funds as income, ABC Corporation establishes a Charitable Scholarship Fund as the means to provide the matching contributions.

ABC Corporation establishes a separate Charitable Foundation, known as the "ABC Corporation Scholarship Foundation" and qualifies the Foundation as a tax-free charitable entity under Internal Revenue Code Section 501(c)(3) (i.e. a charitable organization designed to promote charitable, scientific, literary, educational and religious pursuits). Once the Foundation is qualified as a tax-free entity, ABC Corporation can make the matching contributions into the Foundation. Typically the formation and qualification of a charitable foundation can be achieved within a period of ninety days at a relatively nominal cost to the corporation.

Since the contributions are being made by ABC Corporation to a tax-free charity, the "ABC Corporation Scholarship Foundation," there is no income to be taxed to the employee. When the employee's child reaches college age, the Scholarship Foundation would make a distribution from the College Savings Plan maintained by the Foundation to the child. Again, since the distribution is from a College Savings Plan there is no income to be taxed to the employee or the child.

The rules of the Scholarship Foundation would need to establish some form of standardized benefit to the children of eligible employees. This will ensure that there is a fair means of granting scholarships.

Remember that the rules relating to maximum contribution limits remain even for charitable scholarship funds. For this reason the Foundation can only fund the "ABC Corporation Scholarship Fund's College Savings Account" to the maximum established by the state's laws. Since the Foundation is a charity, the rules do allow for the *re-filling* of the College Savings Account maintained by the Foundation to the state's allowable limit after scholarship awards have been made. In this fashion, a corporation could annually add to the College Savings Account in an amount necessary to fund the year's annual scholarship grants, up to the maximum contribution limit.

For example:

XYZ Corporation establishes a Corporate Sponsored, voluntary College Savings Plan to assist employees with their efforts to save for college expenses. In addition, XYZ Corporation creates a Corporate Scholarship Fund and uses the college Savings Plan as a means to save and invest the Scholarship funds. XYZ Corporation contributes the maximum allowed under the state's laws, $250,000 to the Plan. During 2003, XYZ Corporation makes gifts of $30,000 to employees and their children from the Scholarship Fund. XYZ Corporation is now allowed to *re-fill* the scholarship fund with $30,000 to bring the fund up to the maximum level. ■

Chapter 9

At a Glance

ESTABLISHING A SCHOLARSHIP PROGRAM

✦ Charities can establish College Savings Accounts for purpose of funding scholarships and other charitable endeavors.

✦ College Savings Plans can be used by charities for means to hold and grow assets in a tax deferred/tax free manner for scholarships.

✦ Charities can re-fill the College Savings account back to the state-provided maximum funding level after scholarships have been made to individuals.

UNIVERSITIES AND COLLEGES—COMPENSATION PLANNING

✦ Universities and colleges can use a College Savings Plan as creative compensation tools to provide an education funding benefit to children of employees.

✦ College Savings Plans in the corporate environment can also include "matching" type of contributions by employers into scholarship funds for employees and their children.

CORPORATE-SPONSORED COLLEGE SAVINGS ACCOUNT COMPENSATION PLANNING

✦ Corporations can establish College Savings Accounts as a voluntary corporate benefit for their employees.

THE FUTURE OF
529 PLANS

Research indicates that College Savings Plans will be the single most popular investment vehicle over the next decade. The ability to invest assets on a tax deferred basis, remove the assets tax free, and maintain complete control over the eventual destiny of the account assets, makes the College Savings Plan an extraordinary opportunity.

UPROMISE™ AND BABYMINT™

As the College Savings Plan industry grows, new and interesting approaches to this field will take place. Some are already in progress. Two of the more creative businesses in this field can be found in Upromise™, Inc. and BabyMint™, Inc. Both of these programs are designed to utilize corporate contributions to College Savings Plans on behalf of consumers purchasing the corporation's products. Much like earning free air miles by using an airline sponsored credit card, Upromise™ and BabyMint™ have affiliated themselves with a wide range of corporations that offer free rebate money into a consumer's College Savings Plan. Each company has also affiliated with a credit card issuer, which allows members to earn 1% rebates on their purchases.

The Upromise™ website (**www.Upromise.com**) and the BabyMint™ website (**www.babymint.com**) provide a glimpse into the broad number of corporations offering free contributions to a College Savings Account when purchasing their goods. Upromise™'s partners include, ExxonMobil, AT&T, McDonald's, Staples, 50,000 realtors, 7,000 restaurants, 16,000 grocery stores, over 100 on-line shops, and over 8,500 retail stores.

To obtain the "free" contribution, a consumer logs onto the Upromise™ website and registers one or more credit cards with Upromise™. Once registered, any time a consumer purchases a product with one of the participating businesses using the registered credit card, a contribution is made to a College Savings Account for the consumer's child or family member.

BabyMint™'s business model is slightly different in that BabyMint™ utilizes gift certificates and online purchases with affiliated corporations to generate the contributions to a College Savings Account.

Regardless of where the contributions are deposited, in essence, free money is being contributed to an account for the benefit of someone's college education.

AFFINITY PROGRAMS

The future of College Savings Plans also lies with the *Affinity* type program. Programs such as the Automobile Association of America, American Association of Retired Persons (AARP), Medical and Legal Societies and Associations, and the like will begin to use the College Savings Plan as an added benefit for their membership. Much like the group provided life insurance, auto insurance, travel services, etc., the College Savings Plan will be added to the list of benefits available to association members. These types of College Savings Plans will be more in the nature of the Corporate provided College Savings Plan. It is anticipated that these plans will be priced as an institutional product affording the consumer the opportunity to obtain the College Savings Plan with the least amount of sales and related cost.

The challenge will be to create this opportunity in an environment focused first and foremost on advice and education. Given the broad choices within each different College Savings Plan, and the tax, legal, beneficiary and ownership issues to be grappled with, the Affinity Group provided College Savings Plan will need a strong Advisory group in place to assist with advice and implementation issues.

To date, one group that has taken a lead in the large Corporate and Affinity provided College Savings Plan is Wachovia Securities. By virtue of obtaining selling agreements with many of the Plan Managers, Wachovia Securities has positioned itself to provide the corporate institutional "doorway" through which the large group College Savings Plan can be implemented. The Wachovia Securities model has been built on education and advice first, followed by access to the largest number of available Plan Managers. Through the use of a national call center staffed by experienced investment professionals and national distribution channels, Wachovia Securities seems to be uniquely positioned for the next stage of development of large corporate and affinity provided College Savings Plans.

Chapter 10

At a Glance

THE FUTURE OF 529 PLANS

✦ As the College Savings/529 Plan industry matures, many new and interesting approaches to utilizing the College Savings Plan as an investment vehicle will be created.

✦ Upromise™, Inc. and BabyMint™, Inc. are the first to enter this field with creative strategic relationships with corporations that provided "free" money into a consumer's College Savings Plan account.

AFFINITY PROGRAMS

✦ A natural evolution of the College Savings Plan industry will be towards the large affinity program. Groups such as AAA, AARP, Bar Associations and Medical Societies will begin offering access to College Savings Plan accounts through their membership.

GLOSSARY

A

account owner. The account owner is the person who retains control over who the beneficiary will be and when withdrawals will be made from the College Savings Plan.

advisor plans. 529 Plans that you can obtain through a professional advisor, unlike the retail plan.

age-based investment options. Option where the portfolio is invested based upon the age of the child and the year he or she will be attending college. The longer the time in between now and the time he or she attends college, the more the investments will include stocks and equities. As the child ages and gets closer to the year of college, the investments are shifted more towards income investment and less towards stocks.

B

BabyMint™. A program designed to use corporate contributions to College Savings Plans on behalf of consumers purchasing a particular corporation's products.

beneficiary. The beneficiary is the person who will benefit from the College Savings Plan assets.

C

chase the best return. To try to time the best benefits of the market by jumping in and out of investments.

collateral. Money or property promised in order to get a loan and is used to pay back that loan should the debtor not pay.

College Savings Plan. A College Savings Plan is a plan established and maintained by a state to assist families saving for college. These accounts are also known as Section 529 (of the Internal Revenue Code) plans and offer favorable tax benefits for using the plan to save money for college.

corporate-sponsored College Savings Plan. This is a College Savings Plan that is provided as a voluntary benefit to an employee by his or her employer.

Coverdell Education Savings Accounts. Often referred to as Education IRAs, these are savings/investment accounts into which a person can contribute a maximum of $2,000 per year as of calendar year 2002.

Crummey Trust. A trust that allows for greater control over the principal of the trust for a longer priod of time, by allowing the creator of the trust to stipulate at the time of creation how old a child must be to receive the trust principal.

custodial accounts. A custodial account is an account in which one person holds money or investments for the benefit of another person who is not yet of full age and legal capacity (i.e. UGMA accounts and UTMA accounts).

D

disqualifying distribution. For 529 Plan purposes, removal of money from the 529 Account that is not used for qualified higher education expenses.

E

EGTRRA (Economic Growth and Tax Relief Reconciliation Act of 2001). The law that ensures that no tax is paid on money that is withdrawn from a 529 Plan and used for qualified higher education expenses.

eligible education institution. Any accredited college or graduate school, or post secondary trade or vocational school that can participate in the federal student aid program.

estate taxes. Estate Taxes are taxes charged by the I.R.S. and some states on assets owned by a person at the time of their death.

F

front-end loading. Allowing for more than the annual $11,000 per person gift, so a single person can transfer five times that amount at once ($55,000) to a College Savings Account for a person and not have any amount of the gift reduce their lifetime credit amount.

G

gift tax. A federal tax on the amount given as a gift that exceeds $11,000 per person per year, or $1,000,000 over the lifetime of the gift giver.

H

Hope Scholarship Credit. An income tax credit that has a maximum credit of $1,500 per student each calendar year.

I

institutional approach. To remove the management of investments from the individual to the professional.

irrevocable trusts. An Irrevocable Trust is a trust (set of rules) that can never be changed once created.

K

"Kiddie Tax". Rules that say that all income earned in accounts such as custodial accounts for a child under the age of 14 is taxable to the parent, at the parent's highest income tax bracket. Income earned in these types of accounts are fully taxable to the child, on the child's personal income tax return at the child's income tax rate, once the child is over the age of 14.

L

Lifetime Learning Credit. An income tax credit that has a maximum of $2,000 in calendar year 2002.

M

maximum contribution. The maximum contribution relates to the total amount that may be put aside in a College Savings Plan for one beneficiary.

P

penalty tax. For 529 Plan purposes, an amount equal to 10% of any money withdrawn from a 529 Account that is not used for qualified higher education expenses. This penalty is paid in addition to any regular income taxes on that withdrawl.

Plan Manager. A Plan Manager is the financial services company retained by a state to manage the state's College Savings 529 Plan.

Prepaid Tuition Plan. A Prepaid Tuition Plan is a state-sponsored plan that allows for the purchase of tuition credits for use at state participating colleges.

probate/surrogate law. The laws of a particular state that determine where assets go at the time a person dies if the person did not have a will.

Q

qualified higher education expenses. Qualified higher education expenses is a defined term relating to the expenses for which withdrawals from a College Savings Account are tax free. These include room, board, fees, books, supplies, etc.

Qualified Terminable Interest Property Trust (QTIP). One form of a marital trust, generally for the surviving spouse only, required by tax law to generate income on the principal to the trust.

R

re-filling. The ability to add to an account's funds once a distribution has been made.

retail plans. For purposes of this book, 529 Plans that you can obtain without advice from a professional advisor.

risk-adjusted investments. Investments during a child's younger years that have a higher chance of loss than the investments during the years closer to the child attending college.

S

Section 2503(b) trust. A type of trust created by law, allowing for the saving of assets in an irrevocable trust, with all income earned being distributed to the child. The child pays all income tax on the earnings at the child's or parents' income tax rate, depending on the age of the child. When the child reaches age 25, the trustee must distribute the remaining trust assets outright to the child.

Section 2503(c) trust. A trust specially created by tax law, allowing for the saving of assets in an irrevocable trust, with all income earned being kept in the trust. The trust pays all income tax on the earnings at the trust's income tax rate.

Section 501(C)(3). The code section governing the characteristics to qualify an organization as a charity.

successor owner. The next owner of an account.

"sunset." Legislation coming to an end unless new legislation is passed to keep it alive.

T

tax deferral. Tax deferral relates to the ability to invest assets and have all taxes on income and appreciation held off until sometime in the future.

tax deduction for contributions. This relates to the ability of a person to deduct on their tax return money they have invested on a College Savings Account.

U

UGMA. UGMA refers to the Uniform Gift To Minors Act under which an adult holds assets for the benefit of a minor person.

Upromise^{TM}. A program designed to use corporate contributions to College Savings Plans on behalf of consumers purchasing a particular corporation's products. Much like earning free air miles by using an airline sponsored credit card, Upromise^{TM} has affiliated itself with a wide range of corporations that offer free rebate money into a consumer's College Savings Plan.

UTMA. UTMA refers to Uniform Transfers To Minors Act under which an adults holds assets for the benefit of a minor person.

APPENDIX A

INTERNAL REVENUE CODE SECTION 529

Section 529 Qualified tuition programs.

(a) General rule.

A qualified tuition program shall be exempt from taxation under this subtitle. Notwithstanding the preceding sentence, such program shall be subject to the taxes imposed by section 511 (relating to imposition of tax on unrelated business income of charitable organizations).

(b) Qualified tuition program.

For purposes of this section —

(1) In general. The term "qualified tuition program" means a program established and maintained by a State or agency or instrumentality thereof or by 1 or more eligible educational institutions—

(A) under which a person—

(i) may purchase tuition credits or certificates on behalf of a designated beneficiary which entitle the beneficiary to the waiver or payment of qualified higher education expenses of the beneficiary, or

(ii) in the case of a program established and maintained by a State or agency or instrumentality thereof, may make contributions to an account which is established for the purpose of meeting the qualified higher education expenses of the designated beneficiary of the account, and

(B) which meets the other requirements of this subsection .

Except to the extent provided in regulations, a program established and maintained by 1 or more eligible educational institutions shall not be treated as a qualified tuition program unless such program provides that amounts are held in a qualified trust and such program has received a ruling or determination that such program meets the applicable requirements for a qualified tuition program. For purposes of the preceding sentence, the term "qualified trust" means a trust which is created or organized in the United States for the exclusive benefit of designated beneficiaries and with respect to which the requirements of paragraphs (2) and (5) of section 408(a) are met.

(2) Cash contributions.

A program shall not be treated as a qualified tuition program unless it provides that purchases or contributions may only be made in cash.

(3) Separate accounting.

A program shall not be treated as a qualified tuition program unless it provides separate accounting for each designated beneficiary.

(4) No investment direction.

A program shall not be treated as a qualified tuition program unless it provides that any contributor to, or designated beneficiary under, such program may not directly or indirectly direct the investment of any contributions to the program (or any earnings thereon).

(5) No pledging of interest as security.

A program shall not be treated as a qualified tuition program if it allows any interest in the program or any portion thereof to be used as security for a loan.

(6) Prohibition on excess contributions.

A program shall not be treated as a qualified tuition program unless it provides adequate safeguards to prevent contributions on behalf of a designated beneficiary in excess of those necessary to provide for the qualified higher education expenses of the beneficiary.

(c) Tax treatment of designated beneficiaries and contributors.

(1) In general.

Except as otherwise provided in this subsection, no amount shall be includible in gross income of—

(A) a designated beneficiary under a qualified tuition program, or

(B) a contributor to such program on behalf of a designated beneficiary, with respect to any distribution or earnings under such program.

(2) Gift tax treatment of contributions.

For purposes of chapters 12 and 13—

(A) In general. Any contribution to a qualified tuition program on behalf of any designated beneficiary—

(i) shall be treated as a completed gift to such beneficiary which is not a future interest in property, and

(ii) shall not be treated as a qualified transfer under section 2503(e) .

(B) Treatment of excess contributions. If the aggregate amount of contributions described in subparagraph (A) during the calendar year by a donor exceeds the limitation for such year under section 2503(b) , such aggregate amount shall, at the election of the donor, be taken into account for purposes of such section ratably over the 5-year period beginning with such calendar year.

(3) Distributions.

(A) In general. Any distribution under a qualified tuition program shall be includible in the gross income of the distributee in the manner as provided under section 72 to the extent not excluded from gross income under any other provision of this chapter.

(B) Distributions for qualified higher education expenses. For purposes of this paragraph —

(i) In-kind distributions. No amount shall be includible in gross income under subparagraph (A) by reason of a distribution which consists of providing a benefit to the distributee which, if paid for by the distributee, would constitute payment of a qualified higher education expense.

(ii) Cash distributions. In the case of distributions not described in clause (i) , if—

(I) such distributions do not exceed the qualified higher education expenses (reduced by expenses described in clause (i)), no amount shall be includible in gross income, and

(II) in any other case, the amount otherwise includible in gross income shall be reduced by an amount which bears the same ratio to such amount as such expenses bear to such distributions.

(iii) Exception for institutional programs. In the case of any taxable year beginning before January 1, 2004, clauses (i) and (ii) shall not apply with respect to any distribution during such taxable year under a qualified tuition program established and maintained by 1 or more eligible educational institutions.

(iv) Treatment as distributions. Any benefit furnished to a designated beneficiary under a qualified tuition program shall be treated as a distribution to the beneficiary for purposes of this paragraph.

(v) Coordination with hope and lifetime learning credits. The total amount of qualified higher education expenses with respect to an individual for the taxable year shall be reduced—

(I) as provided in section 25A(g)(2), and

(II) by the amount of such expenses which were taken into account in determining the credit allowed to the taxpayer or any other person under section 25A .

(vi) Coordination with Coverdell education savings accounts. If, with respect to an individual for any taxable year—

(I) the aggregate distributions to which clauses (i) and (ii) and section 530(d)(2)(A) apply, exceed

(II) the total amount of qualified higher education expenses otherwise taken into account under clauses (i) and (ii) (after the application of clause (v)) for such year, the taxpayer shall allocate such expenses among such distributions for purposes of determining the amount of the exclusion under clauses (i) and (ii) and section 530(d)(2)(A).

(C) Change in beneficiaries or programs.

(i) Rollovers. Subparagraph (A) shall not apply to that portion of any distribution which, within 60 days of such distribution, is transferred—

(I) to another qualified tuition program for the benefit of the designated beneficiary, or

(II) to the credit of another designated beneficiary under a qualified tuition program who is a member of the family of the designated beneficiary with respect to which the distribution was made.

(ii) Change in designated beneficiaries. Any change in the designated beneficiary of an interest in a qualified tuition program shall not be treated as a distribution for purposes of subparagraph (A) if the new beneficiary is a member of the family of the old beneficiary.

(iii) Limitation on certain rollovers. Clause (i)(I) shall not apply to any transfer if such transfer occurs within 12 months from the date of a previous transfer to any qualified tuition program for the benefit of the designated beneficiary.

(D) Operating rules. For purposes of applying section 72 —

(i) to the extent provided by the Secretary, all qualified tuition programs of which an individual is a designated beneficiary shall be treated as one program,

(ii) except to the extent provided by the Secretary, all distributions during a taxable year shall be treated as one distribution, and

(iii) except to the extent provided by the Secretary, the value of the contract, income on the contract, and investment in the contract shall be computed as of the close of the calendar year in which the taxable year begins.

(4) Estate tax treatment.

(A) In general. No amount shall be includible in the gross estate of any individual for purposes of chapter 11 by reason of an interest in a qualified tuition program.

(B) Amounts includible in estate of designated beneficiary in certain cases. Subparagraph (A) shall not apply to amounts distributed on account of the death of a beneficiary.

(C) Amounts includible in estate of donor making excess contributions. In the case of a donor who makes the election described in paragraph (2)(B) and who dies before the close of the 5-year period referred to in such paragraph, notwithstanding subparagraph (A), the gross estate of the donor shall include the portion of such contributions properly allocable to periods after the date of death of the donor.

(5) Other gift tax rules.

For purposes of chapters 12 and 13—

(A) Treatment of distributions. Except as provided in subparagraph (B), in no event shall a distribution from a qualified tuition program be treated as a taxable gift.

(B) Treatment of designation of new beneficiary. The taxes imposed by chapters 12 and 13 shall apply to a transfer by reason of a change in the designated beneficiary under the program (or a rollover to the account of a new beneficiary) only if the new beneficiary is a generation below the generation of the old beneficiary (determined in accordance with section 2651).

(6) Additional tax.

The tax imposed by section 530(d)(4) shall apply to any payment or distribution from a qualified tuition program in the same manner as such tax applies to a payment or distribution from an education individual retirement account. This paragraph shall not apply to any payment or distribution in any taxable year beginning before January 1, 2004, which is includible in gross income but used for qualified higher education expenses of the designated beneficiary.

(d) Reports.

Each officer or employee having control of the qualified tuition program or their designee shall make such reports regarding such program to the Secretary and to designated beneficiaries with respect to contributions, distributions, and such other matters as the Secretary may require. The reports required by this subsection shall be filed at such time and in such manner and furnished to such individuals at such time and in such manner as may be required by the Secretary.

(e) Other definitions and special rules.

For purposes of this section —

(1) Designated beneficiary.

The term "designated beneficiary" means—

(A) the individual designated at the commencement of participation in the qualified tuition program as the beneficiary of amounts paid (or to be paid) to the program,

(B) in the case of a change in beneficiaries described in subsection (c)(3)(C), the individual who is the new beneficiary, and

(C) in the case of an interest in a qualified tuition program purchased by a State or local government (or agency or instrumentality thereof) or an organization described in section 501(c)(3) and exempt from taxation under section 501(a) as part of a scholarship program operated by such government or organization, the individual receiving such interest as a scholarship.

(2) Member of family.

The term "member of the family" means, with respect to any designated beneficiary—

(A) the spouse of such beneficiary;

(B) an individual who bears a relationship to such beneficiary which is described in paragraphs (1) through (8) of section 152(a);

(C) the spouse of any individual described in subparagraph (B); and

(D) any first cousin of such beneficiary.

(3) Qualified higher education expenses.

(A) In general. The term "qualified higher education expenses" means—

(i) tuition, fees, books, supplies, and equipment required for the enrollment or attendance of a designated beneficiary at an eligible educational institution; and

(ii) expenses for special needs services in the case of a special needs beneficiary which are incurred in connection with such enrollment or attendance.

(B) Room and board included for students who are at least half-time.

(i) In general. In the case of an individual who is an eligible student (as defined in section 25A(b)(3)) for any academic period, such term shall also include reasonable costs for such period (as determined under the qualified tuition program) incurred by the designated beneficiary for room and board while attending such institution. For purposes of subsection (b)(6) , a designated beneficiary shall be treated as meeting the requirements of this clause.

(ii) Limitation. The amount treated as qualified higher education expenses by reason of clause (i) shall not exceed—

(I) the allowance (applicable to the student) for room and board included in the cost of attendance (as defined in section 472 of the Higher Education Act of 1965 (20 U.S.C. 1087ll), as in effect on the date of the enactment of the Economic Growth and Tax Relief Reconciliation Act of 2001) as determined by the eligible educational institution for such period, or

(II) if greater, the actual invoice amount the student residing in housing owned or operated by the eligible educational institution is charged by such institution for room and board costs for such period.

(4) Application of section 514 .

An interest in a qualified tuition program shall not be treated as debt for purposes of section 514 .

(5) Eligible educational institution.

The term "eligible educational institution" means an institution—

(A) which is described in section 481 of the Higher Education Act of 1965 (20 U.S.C. 1088), as in effect on the date of the enactment of this paragraph, and

(B) which is eligible to participate in a program under title IV of such Act.

APPENDIX B

STATE BY STATE SUMMARY OF PLANS AND PLAN MANAGERS

The following is detailed information for the various College Savings Plans now available in each state. You will see that some states have entered into agreements with more than one Plan Manager, so in these cases there is more than one plan available. Some states have not implemented their College Savings Plan as of the date of publication, and in those cases, none are listed.

ALABAMA

Plan is under development.

ALASKA
Manulife College Savings

Plan Manager	T. Rowe Price and distributed by Manulife Financial
How to reach them	Phone: 1-866-222-7498 Web: www.manulifecollegesavings.com
Annual Fees	$ 30 annual maintenance fee, waived w/automatic deposits or $ 25,000 acct balances. Class A 0.75%, Class C 1.05% (asset-based mgmt fee)
Sales Charges	Class A 3.50% sales load, Class C $ 0 sales load
Underlying Fund Expenses	Approximate range: 0.45% to 1.38%
State Tax Deduction for contribution	No, Alaska has no state income tax
Minimum Investment	$ 500 per portfolio, $ 50 per portfolio for subsequent investments
Maximum Contribution	$ 250,000
Investment Choices	Enrollment-Based Portfolio Fixed Income Portfolio Short-Term Bond Portfolio Equity Portfolio "Future Trends" Portfolio

(continued)

Funds within the Plan's Investment Options

T. Rowe Price Blue Chip Growth

MFS Mass. Investors Gr (Fund A)

T. Rowe Price Value Fund

Davis New York Venture

AIM Aggressive Growth

T. Rowe Price Mid Cap Value

Templeton Foreign

Oppenheimer International Growth

T. Rowe Price Spectrum Income

PIMCO Total Return Bond Fund Admin

T. Rowe Price Summit Cash Reserve

T. Rowe Price Science & Technology Fund

T. Rowe Price Health Sciences Fund

T. Rowe Price Financial Services Fund

Open to Non-Residents   Yes

Can name self as beneficiary   Yes

Date existing Plan Manager contract expires   N/A

(continued)

T. Rowe Price College Saving Plan

Plan Manager   T. Rowe Price

How to reach them   Phone: 1-866-521-1894
                          Web: www.troweprice.com/
                              collegesavings

Annual Fees $30 annual maintenance fee, waived w/auto
                          deposits or with $25,000 acct balance.

                          0.30% (asset-based mgmt fee)

Sales Charges $0

Underlying Fund Expenses   Approximate range: 0.55% to 0.71%

State Tax Deduction   No. Alaska has no state inc tax
for contribution

Minimum Investment $250, $50 w/monthly paymts when using
                          automatic Asset Builder program

Maximum Contribution $250,000

Investment Choices   Age-Based Portfolio Option
                          Equity Option
                          Balanced Option
                          Fixed-Income Option

(continued)

Funds within the Plan's Investment Options	T. Rowe Price Blue Chip Growth
	T. Rowe Price Eq Index 500
	T. Rowe Price Intern'l Stock Fund
	T. Rowe Price Mid-Cap Growth
	T. Rowe Price Small Cap Stock
	T. Rowe Price Value
	T. Rowe Price Spectrum Income
	T. Rowe Price Summit Cash Reserve
	T. Rowe Price U.S. Bond Index
Open to Non-Residents	Yes
Can name self as beneficiary	N/A
Date existing Plan Manager contract expires	N/A

(continued)

University of Alaska College Savings Plan

Plan Manager	T. Rowe Price
How to reach them	Phone: 1-800-478-0003 Web: www.uacollegesavings.com
Annual Fees	$30 annual maintenance fee, waived if you have any money in ACT Portfolio, or with automatic deposits, or $25,000 account balance. 0.30%, waived for ACT Portfolio
Sales Charges	$0
Underlying Fund Expenses range: 0.55% to 0.71% for others	Approx. 0.32% for ACT Portfolio, approx
State Tax Deduction **for contribution**	No. Alaska has no state inc tax
Minimum Investment	$250, $50 with monthly payments when using Automatic Asset Builder program
Maximum Contribution	$250,000
Investment Choices	Enrollment-Based Portfolio Option Equity Portfolio Balanced POrtfolio Fixed-Income Portfolio ACT Portfolio (30% stock funds)

(continued)

Funds within the Plan's   (ALL T. Rowe Price funds)

Investment Options   U.S. Bond Index

Equity Index

Summit Cash Reserves

Spectrum Income

Blue Chip Growth

Value

Mid-Cap

Small-Cap Stock

International Stock

Open to Non-Residents   Yes

Can name self as beneficiary   Yes

Date existing Plan Manager   12/31/2016

contract expires

ARIZONA

Arizona Family College Savings Program

Plan Manager   College Savings Bank

How to reach them   Phone: 800-888-2723
                                          Web: www.collegesavings.com

Annual Fees   0.0%

Sales Charges $0

State Tax Deduction   No
for contribution

Minimum Investment $250, or $25 per pay period for payroll deduction
                                          deposits, or $100 per mo. for automatic transfers
                                          from a bank acct.

Maximum Contribution $177,000

Investment Choices   CollegeSure Certificates of Deposit

Funds within the Plan's   0
Investment Options

Open to Non-Residents   Yes

Can name self as beneficiary   Yes

Date existing Plan Manager   N/A
contract expires

(continued)

Arizona Family College Savings Program

Plan Manager   Securities Mgmt & Research, Inc.

How to reach them   Phone: 888-66-READY
                                     Web: www.smrinvest.com

Annual Fees   0.0%

Sales Charges $10 enrollment per mutual fund

Underlying Fund Expenses   Approx range: 0.49% to 2.10%

State Tax Deduction   No
for contribution

Minimum Investment $20 to $500 per fund depending on fund and frequency

Maximum Contribution $177,000

Investment Choices   10 mutual funds (below)

Funds within the Plan's   SM&R Alger Technology Fund
Investment Options   SM&R Alger Aggr. Growth Fund
                                     SM&R Alger Small-Cap Fund
                                     SM&R Alger Growth Fund
                                     SM&R Growth Fund
                                     SM&R Equity Income Fund
                                     SM&R Balanced Fund
                                     SM&R Government Bond Fund
                                     SM&R Primary Fund
                                     SM&R Money Market Fund

(continued)

Open to Non-Residents	Yes
Can name self as beneficiary	N/A
Date existing Plan Manager contract expires	N/A

(continued)

Waddell & Reed InvestEd Plan

Plan Manager   Waddell & Reed

How to reach them   Phone: 888-WADDELL
Web: www.waddell.com

Annual Fees   A shares: 0.91%
B shares: 1.66%

Sales Charges $10 enrollment fee
A shares: 5.75% sales load
B or C shares: contingent deferred sales

charges

Underlying Fund Expenses   Approx range: 0.79% to 0.92%

State Tax Deduction   No
for contribution

Minimum Investment $500 lump sum, $50 automatic investment plan, or
$25 payroll deduction

Maximum Contribution $177,000

Investment Choices   InvestEd Balanced Portfolio
InvestEd Conservative Portfolio
InvestEd Growth Portfolio

(continued)

Funds within the Plan's Investment Options	Advisors Core Investment
	Advisors Value
	Advisors International Growth
	Advisors Vanguard
	Advisors New Concepts
	Advisors Small Cap
	Advisors Bond Fund
	Advisors Government Securities
	Advisors High Income
	Advisors Cash Management
Open to Non-Residents	Yes
Can name self as beneficiary	N/A
Date existing Plan Manager contract expires	N/A

ARKANSAS

GIFT College Investing Plan

Plan Manager	Mercury Funds
How to reach them	Phone: 1-877-442-6553
	Web: www.thegiftplan.com
Annual Fees	$25, annual maint. fee, waived for residents and $25K+ acct balance
	0.60% (asset-based mgmt fee)
Sales Charges	$0
Underlying Fund Expenses	0.70% to 1.38%
State Tax Deduction for contribution	No
Minimum Investment	$250 for residents, $1,000 for non-residents
Maximum Contribution	$245,000
Investment Choices	Age-Based Portfolio Option
	Growth Option
	Growth and Income Option
	Balanced Option
	Fixed-Income Option

(continued)

Funds within the Plan's Investment Options

Mercury Large Cap Core Fund

Franklin Blue Chip Fund

Mercury Growth Opportunity

Franklin Equity Income Fund

Mercury U.S. SmallCap Growth

Franklin Balance Sheet Investment FundMutual
    Shares Fund

Mercury International Fund

Templeton Foreign Fund

Mercury Aggregate Bond Index

Franklin Total Return Fund

Mercury U.S. High Yield

Summit Cash Reserves

Open to Non-Residents

Yes

Can name self as beneficiary

N/A

Date existing Plan Manager contract expires

N/A

CALIFORNIA

Golden State ScholarShare

Plan Manager	TIAA-CREF Life Ins. Co.
How to reach them	Phone: 1-877-SAV-4-EDU
	Web: www.scholarshare.com
Annual Fees	0.7%-0.8% (asset-based mgmt fee)
Sales Charges	$0
Underlying Fund Expenses	Included in asset-based mgmt fee
State Tax Deduction for contribution	No
Minimum Investment	$25 per investment option or $15 per investment opt per pay period
Maximum Contribution	$124,799 to $174,648
Investment Choices	Age-Based Asset Allocation Opt.
	Aggr. Age-Based Asset Alloc. Opt.
	100% Equity Option
	100% Social Choice Option
	Guaranteed Option

(continued)

Funds within the Plan's Investment Options	Growth Equity Fund
	Growth and Income Fund
	Social Choice Equity Fund
	International Equity Fund
	Bond Fund
	Money Market Fund
	Equity Index
Open to Non-Residents	Yes
Can name self as beneficiary	Yes
Date existing Plan Manager contract expires	10/21/2006

COLORADO

CollegeInvest/Scholars Choice College Savings Program

Plan Manager	Salomon Smith Barney
How to reach them	Phone: 1-888-572-4652 Web: www.scholars-choice.com
Annual Fees	$30 annual maintenance fee for non-Colorado residents 0.99% to 1.09% service fee for direct-sold account
Sales Charges	$0 for direct-sold
Underlying Fund Expenses accounts	Included in service fee for direct-sold
State Tax Deduction for contribution	Yes
Minimum Investment	$25, and subsequent contribs must be $15+; no min contribs if paid by payroll deduction deposits
Maximum Contribution	$235,000
Investment Choices	Age-Based Portfolio Option 100% Equity Option Balanced Option Fixed Income Option

(continued)

Funds within the Plan's Investment Options	Salomon Bros Investor Value Fund
	Smith Barney LargeCap Gr Fund
	Smith Barn. SmallCap Core Fund
	AFG Euro Pacific Growth Fund
	Smith Barney Investment Grade Bond Fund
	MFS Government Securities
	Smith Barney Short-Term High Grade Bond
	Smith Barney Cash Portfolio
Open to Non-Residents	Yes
Can name self as beneficiary	N/A
Date existing Plan Manager contract expires	N/A

CONNECTICUT

Connecticut Higher Education Trust (CHET)

Plan Manager	TIAA-CREF
How to reach them	Phone: 1-888-799-CHET Web: www.aboutchet.com
Annual Fees	0.57% to 0.59% (asset-based mgmt fee)
Sales Charges	$0
Underlying Fund Expenses	Approximate range: 0.16% to 0.22%
State Tax Deduction for contribution	No
Minimum Investment	$25, $15 per pay period for payroll deduction deposits
Maximum Contribution	$235,000
Investment Choices	Age-Based Portfolio Plan High Equity Option Guaranteed Option
Funds within the Plan's Investment Options	TIAA-CREF Inst. Eq Index Fund TIAA-CREF Inst. Gr & Inc Fund TIAA-CREF Inst. Intern'l Eq Fund TIAA-CREF Inst. Bond Fund TIAA-CREF Inst. Money Mkt Fund
Open to Non-Residents	Yes
Can name self as beneficiary	N/A
Date existing Plan Manager contract expires	N/A

DELAWARE

Delaware College Investment Plan

Plan Manager	Fidelity Investments
How to reach them	Phone: 1-800-544-1655 Web: www.fidelity.com/delaware
Annual Fees	$30 annual maintenance fee, waived w/auto deposits or $25,000 acct balances 0.30% (asset-based mgmt fee)
Sales Charges	$0
Underlying Fund Expenses	Approx range: 0.65% to 0.81%
State Tax Deduction **for contribution**	No
Minimum Investment	$500 and subsequent contributions must be $50+
Maximum Contribution	$250,000
Investment Choices	Age-Based Portfolio Option 100% Equity 70% Equity

(continued)

Funds within the Plan's   (ALL Fidelity mutual funds)

Investment Options   Blue Chip Growth

Disciplined Equity

Equity-Income

Fidelity Fund

Growth & Income Portfolio

Growth Company

OTC Portfolio

Diversified International Overseas

Government Income

Intermediate Bond

Investment Grade Bond

Capital & Income

Daily Income

Short-Term Bond

Open to Non-Residents   Yes

Can name self as beneficiary   N/A

Date existing Plan Manager   N/A
contract expires

FLORIDA

Florida College Savings Plan

Plan is under development and set to launch in late 2002.

GEORGIA

Georgia Higher Education Savings Plan

Plan Manager	TIAA-CREF
How to reach them	Phone: 1-877-424-4377
	Web: www.gacollegesavings.com
Annual Fees	0.85% (asset-based mgmt fee)
Sales Charges	$0
Underlying Fund Expenses	Included in asset-based mgmt fee
State Tax Deduction for contribution	Yes
Minimum Investment	$25,
	$15
	through an automatic investment plan
Maximum Contribution	$235,000
Investment Choices	Managed Allocation Option
	Aggr Managed Allocation Option
	100% Equity
	Balanced Fund
	Guaranteed
Funds within the Plan's Investment Options	N/A
Open to Non-Residents	Yes
Can name self as beneficiary	N/A
Date existing Plan Manager contract expires	N/A

HAWAII

TuitionEDGE

Plan Manager	Delaware Investments
How to reach them	Phone: 1-866-529-3343 Web: www.tuitionedge.com
Annual Fees	$25 ann maint fee (waived for accts over $10,000 and HI residents) 0.95% (asset-based mgmt fee)
Sales Charges	$0
Underlying Fund Expenses	included in asset-based mgmt fee
State Tax Deduction for contribution	No
Minimum Investment	$15 per investment option
Maximum Contribution	$253,000
Investment Choices	Age-Based Option Conservative Aggressive Balanced Savings Account Option (w/First Hawaiian Bank)
Funds within the Plan's Investment Options	N/A
Open to Non-Residents	Yes
Can name self as beneficiary	N/A
Date existing Plan Manager contract expires	N/A

IDAHO
Idaho College Savings Program (Ideal)

Plan Manager	TIAA-CREF
How to reach them	Phone: 1-866-433-2533
	Web: www.idsaves.org
Annual Fees	0.70% (asset-based mgmt fee)
Sales Charges	$0
Underlying Fund Expenses	Approximate range: 0.16% to 0.23%
State Tax Deduction for contribution	Yes
Minimum Investment	$25, $15 per pay period for payroll deduction deposits
Maximum Contribution	$235,000
Investment Choices	Age-Based Portfolio Option
	100% Equity
	Money Market
Funds within the Plan's Investment Options	TIAA-CREF Inst. Growth Equity Fund
	TIAA-CREF Inst. Gr & Inc Fund
	TIAA-CREF Inst. International Equity Fund
	TIAA-CREF Inst. Bond Fund
	TIAA-CREF Inst. Money Market Fund
Open to Non-Residents	Yes
Can name self as beneficiary	N/A
Date existing Plan Manager contract expires	N/A

ILLINOIS

Bright Start College Savings Program

Plan Manager   Salomon Smith Barney

How to reach them   Phone: 1-877-43-BRIGHT
Web: www.brightstartsavings.com

Annual Fees   0.99% (asset-based mgmt fee)

Sales Charges $30 application fee if opened through a bank

Underlying Fund Expenses Included in (asset-based mgmt fee)

State Tax Deduction
for contribution   Yes

Minimum Investment $25 initial, subsequent must be $115

Maximum Contribution $235,000

Investment Choices   Age-Based Investment Option
Fixed Income Option
Equity Investment Option

(continued)

Funds within the Plan's Investment Options	Large Cap Value Fund
	Large Cap Growth Fund
	Small Cap Core Fund
	International All Cap Growth
	Investment Grade Bond Fund
	Managed Government Funds
	Short-term High Grade Bond
	Cash Portfolio
Open to Non-Residents	Yes
Can name self as beneficiary	Yes
Date existing Plan Manager contract expires	N/A

INDIANA

CollegeChoice 529 Plan

Plan Manager	One Group Investments
How to reach them	Phone: 1-866-400-7526 Web: www.collegechoiceplan.com
Annual Fees	$10 annual maintenance fee for resident, $30 for non-resident, or $25 for any account converted from former Indiana 529 plan. Fee waived w/$25,000 balances or w/auto contributions. Non-residents also incur $10 annual state authority fee. Structure A 0.40%, Structure B 0.95%, Structure C 0.65% (asset-based mgmt fee)
Sales Charges	$0, except fee Structure A includes 3.5% initial sales charge
Underlying Fund Expenses	0.35% to 0.97%
State Tax Deduction for contribution	No
Minimum Investment	$50 initial, subsequent must be more than $25
Maximum Contribution	$114,548 (increasing to $236,750 on 07/01/02)

(continued)

Investment Choices

Age-Based Portfolio Plan

Equity Index Portfolio

Growth Portfolio

Growth & Income Portfolio

Balanced Portfolio

Conservative Growth Portfolio

Tuition Portfolio

Bond Portfolio

Funds within the Plan's Investment Options

N/A

Open to Non-Residents

Yes

Can name self as beneficiary

N/A

Date existing Plan Manager contract expires

N/A

IOWA

College Savings Iowa

Plan Manager	State Treasurer and The Vanguard Group
How to reach them	Phone: 888-672-9116 Web:www.collegesavingsiowa.com
Annual Fees	0.65% (ann. asset-base mgmt fee)
Sales Charges	$0
Underlying Fund Expenses	Included in (asset-based mgmt fee)
State Tax Deduction for contribution	Yes
Minimum Investment	$25 min initial, and $50 min per yr
Maximum Contribution	$146,000
Investment Choices	4 "savings tracks" that range in asset allocations. No "static" investment options available.
Funds within the Plan's Investment Options	Vanguard Institutional Index Fund Vanguard Extended Mkt Index Fund–Inst. Shares Vanguard Inst. Developed Mkts Index Fund Vanguard Total Bond Mkt Index Fund–Inst. Shares
Open to Non-Residents	Yes
Can name self as beneficiary	N/A
Date existing Plan Manager contract expires	N/A

KANSAS

Learning Quest Education Savings Program

Plan Manager	American Century
How to reach them	Phone: 1-800-579-2203
	Web: www.learningquestsavings.com
Annual Fees	$40 annual maintenance fee ($10 for accounts with $100K+ balance, $0 for Kansas residents)
	0.39% (asset-based mgmt fee)
Sales Charges	$0
Underlying Fund Expenses	Approximate range: 0.52% to 0.95%
State Tax Deduction for contribution	Yes
Minimum Investment	$500 initial, or $2,500 for non-Kansas residents. Subsequent contributions must be more than $50
Maximum Contribution	$235,000
Investment Choices	Age-Based Portfolio Option
	Aggressive
	Moderate
	Conservative

(continued)

**Funds within the Plan's
Investment Options**

American Century Growth Fund

American Century Select Fund

American Century Vista Fund

American Century Heritage

American Century Inc & Gr Fund

American Century Eq Growth Fund

Am. Cent. Large Cap Value Fund

American Century Value Fund

American Century Eq Inc Fund

American Century Intern'l Gr Fund

Am. Century Premium Bond Fund

Am. Cent. Prem. Cap Reserve Fund

Open to Non-Residents   Yes

Can name self as beneficiary   N/A

**Date existing Plan Manager
contract expires**   N/A

KENTUCKY

Kentucky Education Savings Plan Trust

Plan Manager	TIAA-CREF
How to reach them	Phone: 1-877-598-7878
	Web: www.kentuckytrust.com
Annual Fees	0.81% (asset-based mgmt fee)
Sales Charges	$0
Underlying Fund Expenses	Incl. in asset-based mgmt fee
State Tax Deduction for contribution	No
Minimum Investment	Initial and subsequent contribution amount is $25, $15 per pay period for payroll deduction deposits
Maximum Contribution	$235,000
Investment Choices	Age-Based Portfolio
	100% Equity
Funds within the Plan's Investment Options	TIAA-CREF Inst. Gr Eq Fund
	TIAA-CREF Inst. Gr & Inc Fund
	TIAA-CREF Inst. Intern'l Eq Fund
	TIAA-CREF Inst. Bond Fund
	TIAA-CREF Inst. Money Mkt Fund
Open to Non-Residents	No
Can name self as beneficiary	N/A
Date existing Plan Manager contract expires	N/A

LOUISIANA

Student Tuition Assistance and Revenue Trust Program (START)

Plan Manager	self-managed
How to reach them	Phone: 1-800-259-5626 Web: www.osfa.state.la.us/start.htm
Annual Fees	$0
Sales Charges	$0
Underlying Fund Expenses	$0
State Tax Deduction for contribution	Yes
Minimum Investment	Minimum initial and subsequent amount is $10
Maximum Contribution	$173,065
Investment Choices	Fixed Income static investment opt
Funds within the Plan's Investment Options	N/A
Open to Non-Residents	No. Account owner or beneficiary must be LA resident
Can name self as beneficiary	N/A
Date existing Plan Manager contract expires	N/A

MAINE

NextGen College Investing Plan

Plan Manager Merrill Lynch

How to reach them Phone: 1-877-463-9843
Web: www.nextgenplan.com

Annual Fees $50 annual maintenance fee waived if:
i) account owner or beneficiary is a Maine resident; ii) annual contributions are $2,500 or more; or, iii) the account value is $20,000 or more at the end of the fee year.

0.55% asset based management fee in Client Direct series; 0.71% to 1.79% in Client Adviser series avail through brokers

Sales Charges $0

Underlying Fund Expenses Approx range: 0.76% to 0.95% in Client Direct series; 0.71% to 1.79% in Client Adviser series

State Tax Deduction for contribution No

Minimum Investment $250 initial lump sum, or $50 per month for payroll deduction deposit or auto bank transfer

Maximum Contribution $235,000

(continued)

Investment Choices

Age-Based Portfolio Plan

3 other options in Client Direct series

100% Equity

75% Equity

Fixed Income

11 options available in Client Adviser series

Funds within the Plan's Investment Options

N/A

Open to Non-Residents

Yes

Can name self as beneficiary

N/A

Date existing Plan Manager contract expires

N/A

MARYLAND

College Savings Plan of Maryland – College Investment Plan

Plan Manager	T. Rowe Price
How to reach them	Phone: 1-888-463-4723 Web: www.collegesavingsmd.com
Annual Fees	$30 annual maintenance fee, waived for auto invest plan or $25K+ balance. Up to 0.38% (asset-based mgmt fee)
Sales Charges	$90 enrollment fee (reduced under certain conditions)
Underlying Fund Expenses	Range of fund expenses 0.35% to 0.99%
State Tax Deduction for contribution	Yes
Minimum Investment	$250 initial lump sum, or min $25 per month automatic contributions
Maximum Contribution	$175,000
Investment Choices	Age-Based Portfolio Plan 100% Equity 100% Bond Balanced
Funds within the Plan's Investment Options	N/A
Open to Non-Residents	Yes
Can name self as beneficiary	N/A
Date existing Plan Manager contract expires	N/A

MASSACHUSETTS

U.Fund College Investing Plan

Plan Manager   Fidelity Investments

How to reach them   Phone: 1-800-544-2776
                            Web: www.mefa.org

Annual Fees $30 annual maintenance fee, waived w/auto
                            deposits or more than $25,000 account balances.

                            0.30% (asset-based mgmt fee)

Sales Charges $0

Underlying Fund Expenses   Approximate range: 0.64% to 0.81%

State Tax Deduction   No
for contribution

Minimum Investment $1,000 initial lump sum, or $50 per month for pay-
                            roll deduction deposits or auto bank transfer

Maximum Contribution $230,000

Investment Choices   Age-Based Portfolio Plan
                            100% Equity
                            70% Equity

(continued)

**Funds within the Plan's
Investment Options**

(ALL Fidelity mutual funds)

Blue Chip Growth

Disciplined Equity

Dividend Growth

Equity-Income Fund

Equity-Income II

Fidelity Fund

Growth and Income Portfolio

Growth Company

OTC Portfolio

Spartan 500 Index Fund

Diversified International Overseas

Government Income

Intermediate Bond

Investment Grade Bond

Capital & Income

Daily Income Trust

Short-Term Bond

Open to Non-Residents   Yes

Can name self as beneficiary   N/A

**Date existing Plan Manager
contract expires**   N/A

MICHIGAN

Michigan Education Savings Program

Plan Manager	TIAA-CREF
How to reach them	Phone: 1-877-861-MESP Web: www.misaves.com
Annual Fees	0.65% (asset-based mgmt fee)
Sales Charges	$0
Underlying Fund Expenses	Incl. in asset-based mgmt fee
State Tax Deduction for contribution	Yes
Minimum Investment	$25, $15 per pay period for payroll deduction deposits
Maximum Contribution	$235,000
Investment Choices	Age-Based Portfolio Plan 100% Equity Option Guaranteed Investment Option
Funds within the Plan's Investment Options	N/A
Open to Non-Residents	Yes
Can name self as beneficiary	N/A
Date existing Plan Manager contract expires	N/A

MINNESOTA

Minnesota College Savings Plan

Plan Manager	TIAA-CREF
How to reach them	Phone: 1-877-338-4646 Web: www.mnsaves.org
Annual Fees	0.65% annual (asset-based mgmt fee)
Sales Charges	$0
Underlying Fund Expenses	Incl. in asset-based mgmt fee
State Tax Deduction for contribution	No
Minimum Investment	$25, $15 for payroll deduction deposits
Maximum Contribution	$122,484
Investment Choices	Age-Based Portfolio Plan 100% Equity Guaranteed Option (min return of 3%)
Funds within the Plan's Investment Options	TIAA-CREF Inst. Eq. Index Fund TIAA-CREF Inst. Gr & Inc Fund TIAA-CREF Inst. Intern'l Eq. Fund TIAA-CREF Inst. Bond Fund TIAA-CREF Inst. Money Mkt Fund
Open to Non-Residents	Yes
Can name self as beneficiary	N/A
Date existing Plan Manager contract expires	N/A

MISSISSIPPI

Mississippi Affordable College Savings Program

Plan Manager	TIAA-CREF Tuition Financing, Inc.
How to reach them	Phone: 800-486-3670 Web: www.collegesavingsms.com
Annual Fees	0.7% (asset-based mgmt fee)
Sales Charges	$0
Underlying Fund Expenses	Approximate range: 0.16% to 0.23%
State Tax Deduction for contribution	Yes
Minimum Investment	$25 initial and subsequent min per invest. opt., or $15 per investment opt. per payroll period using payroll deduction
Maximum Contribution	$235,000
Investment Choices	Managed Allocation Option Money Market Option 100% Equity Option

(continued)

Funds within the Plan's	TIAA-CREF Inst. Internatioinal Equity Fund
Investment Options	TIAA-CREF Inst. Growth & Income Fund
	TIAA-CREF Inst. Bond Fund
	TIAA-CREF Inst. Money Mkt Fund
Open to Non-Residents	Yes
Can name self as beneficiary	No
Date existing Plan Manager contract expires	01/01/2012

MISSOURI

Missouri Saving for Tuition Program (MO$T)

Plan Manager	TIAA-CREF
How to reach them	Phone: 1-888-414-6678 Web: www.missourimost.org
Annual Fees	0.65% (asset-based mgmt fee)
Sales Charges	$0
Underlying Fund Expenses	Included in (asset-based mgmt fee)
State Tax Deduction for contribution	Yes
Minimum Investment	$25, $15 for payroll deduction deposits
Maximum Contribution	$235,000
Investment Choices	Managed Allocation Option 100% Equity Option Guaranteed Principal Plus Interest (w/an annual min return of 3%)
Funds within the Plan's Investment Options	TIAA-CREF Inst. Growth Eq. Fund TIAA-CREF Inst. Int'l Equity Fund TIAA-CREF Inst. Gr & Inc Fund TIAA-CREF Inst. Bond Fund TIAA-CREF Inst. Money Mkt Fund
Open to Non-Residents	Yes
Can name self as beneficiary	N/A
Date existing Plan Manager contract expires	05/2004

MONTANA

Montana Family Education Savings Program

Plan Manager	College Savings Bank
How to reach them	Phone: 1-800-888-2723 Web: http://montana.collegesavings.com
Annual Fees	$0
Sales Charges	$0
Underlying Fund Expenses	$0
State Tax Deduction for contribution	Yes
Minimum Investment	$250, $25 for payroll deduction deposits, $100 per month or $250 per quarter for automatic bank transfer
Maximum Contribution	$177,000
Investment Choices	FDIC-insured certificate of deposit
Funds within the Plan's Investment Options	N/A
Open to Non-Residents	Yes
Can name self as beneficiary	Yes
Date existing Plan Manager contract expires	N/A

NEBRASKA

AIM College Savings Plan

Plan Manager	Union Bank and AIM
How to reach them	Phone: 1-877-246-7526 Web: www.aimfunds.com
Annual Fees	$25 annual maintenance fee, waived for account balances of more than $50,000 ($25,000 if in automatic investment plan) 0.35% for Class A shares, 0.90% for Class B and C shares ((asset-based mgmt fee))
Sales Charges	$0 (3.5% sales load for Class A shares)
Underlying Fund Expenses	Approximate range: 1.06% to 1.67%
State Tax Deduction for contribution	Yes
Minimum Investment	$500 per portfolio w/subsequent of $50, or $50 for automatic enrollment plan with subsequent of $25
Maximum Contribution	$250,000
Investment Choices	Enrollment-Based Portfolio Aggressive Growth Portfolio Growth Portfolio Balanced Portfolio

(continued)

**Funds within the Plan's
Investment Options**

AIM Basic Value Fund

AIM Blue Chip Fund

AIM Constellation Fund

AIM Mid Cap Equity Fund

AIM Small Cap Growth Fund

AIM International Value Fund

AIM International Equity Fund

AIM Intermediate Equity Fund

AIM Intermediate Govt. Fund

AIM Money Market Fund

Open to Non-Residents   Yes

Can name self as beneficiary   Yes

**Date existing Plan Manager
contract expires**   N/A

(continued)

College Savings Plan of Nebraska

Plan Manager   Union Bank and Trust

How to reach them   Phone: 1-888-993-3746
Web: www.planforcollegenow.com

Annual Fees $24 annual maintenance fee

0.60% asset-based mgmt fee for direct sold accounts

Sales Charges $0

Underlying Fund Expenses Approximate range: 0.32% to 0.44%

**State Tax Deduction
for contribution**   Yes

Minimum Investment No minimum

Maximum Contribution $250,000

Investment Choices   Age-Based Portfolios
Aggressive
Growth
Balanced
Conservative
6 static investment options

(continued)

Funds within the Plan's Investment Options	State Street 500
	Vanguard Extended Market Index
	American Century Inc & Growth
	Fidelity Advisors Equity Growth
	American Century Equity Income
	Janus Enterprise
	Vanguard Total Int'l Stock Index
	Fidelity Diversified International
	T. Rowe Price Foreign Equity Fund
	PIMCO Total Return Fund
	Vanguard Total Bond Market Index
	Vanguard Prime Money Market
Open to Non-Residents	Yes
Can name self as beneficiary	N/A
Date existing Plan Manager contract expires	N/A

NEVADA
America's College Savings Plan

Plan Manager	Strong Capital
How to reach them	Phone: 1-877-529-5295 Web: www.americas529plan.com
Annual Fees	$25 annual maintenance fee waived w/$25,000 or more balance or enrollment in auto invest plan or payroll deduction 1.30% annual asset-based mgmt fee
Sales Charges	$25 enrollment fee
Underlying Fund Expenses	Included in (asset-based mgmt fee)
State Tax Deduction for contribution	No
Minimum Investment	$250 lump sum, or $50 per month auto investment plan
Maximum Contribution	$246,000
Investment Choices	Age-Based Plan Aggressive Portfolio Moderate Portfolio Conservative Portfolio

(continued)

Funds within the Plan's   (All Strong funds)

Investment Options   Growth Fund

                                    Advisor U.S. Value (Class Z)

                                    Opportunity Fund

                                    Advisor SmallCap Value Fund

                                    Corporate Bond Fund

                                    Government Securities Fund

                                    Advantage Fund

                                    Short-Term Bond Fund

Open to Non-Residents   Yes

Can name self as beneficiary   N/A

Date existing Plan Manager   N/A
contract expires

(continued)

American Skandia College Savings Program

Plan Manager	Strong Capital Management and American Skandia
How to reach them	Phone: 1-800-SKANDIA Web: www.americanskandia.com
Annual Fees	$30 annual maintenance fee, waived for $25,000 or more acct balance or enrollment in auto investment plan Asset-based mgmt fee: A shares 0.15% annual fee, C shares 0.60% annual fee, and 1% contingent deferred sales charge for non-qual withdrawal or rollover w/in 2 yrs of contribution
Sales Charges	$0. Class A shares have 3.50% initial sales charge
Underlying Fund Expenses	Approximate range: 0.94% to 2.20%
State Tax Deduction for contribution	No
Minimum Investment	$250 initial, $50 w/auto investment plan. Subsequent contributions must be $50 or more
Maximum Contribution	$246,000

(continued)

Investment Choices

Age-Based Portfolio Options

Aggressive

Moderate

Conservative

Aggressive Option

Balanced Option

Conservative Option

Funds within the Plan's
Investment Options

ASAF PBGH SmCap Growth Fund

ASAF Gabelli SmCap Value Fund

ASAF Neuberger Berman MidCap Growth Fund

ASAF Gabelli All-Cap Value Fund

ASAF Marsico Cap. Growth Fund

ASAF Invesco Equity Inc Fund

ASAF Federated High Yield Bond Fund

ASAF Pimco Total Return Bond Fund

ASAF Money Market Fund

ASAF Strong Internatl Equity Fund

Strong Govt. Securities

Strong Corporate Bond

Open to Non-Residents

Yes

Can name self as beneficiary

N/A

Date existing Plan Manager
contract expires

N/A

New Hampshire

The Advisor College Investing Plan

Plan Manager	Fidelity Investments
How to reach them	Phone: 1-800-522-7297 Web: www.advisorxpress.com
Annual Fees	$30 annual maintenance fee, waived for 25,000 or more balance or auto contributions 0.30% (asset-based mgmt fee), plus 0.25% (class A shares), 0.75% (class B shares), or 0.50% (class c). Class B shares subject to contingent deferred sales charge w/in 6 yrs of contribution.
Sales Charges	$0, except Class A shares have a 3.50% initial sales charge
Underlying Fund Expenses	Approximate range: 0.48% to 1.24%
State Tax Deduction for contribution	No
Minimum Investment	$1,000 ($50 for auto investment plan)
Maximum Contribution	$233,240
Investment Choices	Age-Based Portfolio 100% Equity Portfolio 70% Equity Portfolio
Funds within the Plan's Investment Options	N/A
Open to Non-Residents	Yes
Can name self as beneficiary	N/A
Date existing Plan Manager contract expires	N/A

UNIQUE College Investing Plan

Plan Manager	Fidelity Investments
How to reach them	Phone: 1-800-544-1722 Web: www.fidelity.com/unique
Annual Fees	$30, waived w/auto deposits or more than $25,000 account balances. 0.30% (asset-based mgmt fee)
Sales Charges	$0
Underlying Fund Expenses	Approximate range: 0.65% to 0.81%
State Tax Deduction for contribution	No
Minimum Investment	$1,000 initial, or $50 per month for auto bank transfers or payroll deduction deposit
Maximum Contribution	$233, 240
Investment Choices	Age-Based Portfolio 100% Equity Option 70% Equity Option

(continued)

Funds within the Plan's
Investment Options

Fidelity Blue Chip Growth

Fidelity Disciplined Equity

Fidelity Equity-Income Fund

Fidelity Fund

Fidelity Gr & Inc Portfolio

Fidelity Growth Co.

Fidelity OTC Portfolio

Fidelity Diversified Internatl

Fidelity Overseas

Fidelity Govt. Income

Fidelity Intermed. Bond

Fidelity Investment Grade Bond

Fidelity Capital & Income

Fidelity Daily Income Trust

Fidelity Short-Term Bond

Open to Non-Residents   Yes

Can name self as beneficiary   N/A

Date existing Plan Manager   N/A
contract expires

NEW JERSEY

New Jersey Better Educational Savings Trust

Plan Manager   Dept. of the Treasury, Division of Investment

How to reach them   Phone: 1-877-4NJBEST
                                        Web: www.hesaa.org

Annual Fees $5 annual maintenance fee

                                        0.50% (asset-based mgmt fee)

Sales Charges $0

State Tax Deduction   No
for contribution

Minimum Investment $25 per month and $300 annual
                                        until acct reaches $1,200

Maximum Contribution $185,000

Investment Choices   Age-based investment program

Funds within the Plan's   0
Investment Options

Open to Non-Residents   No

Can name self as beneficiary   Yes

Date existing Plan Manager   N/A
contract expires

NEW MEXICO

CollegeSense 529 Higher Education Savings Plan

Plan Manager	Schoolhouse Capital and New York Life Investment Management
How to reach them	Phone: 1-866-529-7367 Web: www.collegesense.com
Annual Fees	$25 annual maintenance fee, waived: i) w/auto deposits; ii) $25,000 or more account balance; or, iii) account owner or beneficiary is NM resident 0.35% (asset-based mgmt fee) plus distrib expenses that vary based on share class
Sales Charges	$0, except A shares incur a sales load
Underlying Fund Expenses	N/A
State Tax Deduction for contribution	Yes
Minimum Investment	$250 initial lump sum, or $25 per month or $75 per quarter
Maximum Contribution	$251,000

(continued)

Investment Choices	Age-Based Portfolio
	100% Equity Option
	100% Bond Option
	100% Short-Term Yield
	5 blended portfolios
Funds within the Plan's	MainStay Capital Apprec. Fund A
Investment Options	SSGA Growth & Income Fund
	MainStay Value Fund A
	JP Morgan Capital Growth Fund A
	JP Morgan Capital Dynamic
	SmallCap Fund A
	MainStay Internatl Equity Fund A
	SSGA Internatl Growth Opportunities Fund
	Eclipse Core Bond Plus Fund
	SSGA Bond Market Fund
	Eclipse Money Mkt Fund Service
Open to Non-Residents	Yes
Can name self as beneficiary	N/A
Date existing Plan Manager contract expires	N/A

(continued)

171

The Education Plan's College Savings Program

Plan Manager	Schoolhouse Capital
How to reach them	Phone: 1-877-EDPLAN8 Web: www.theeducationplan.com
Annual Fees	$30 annual maintenance fee, waived: i) w/auto deposits; ii) $10,000 or more account balance; or, iii) account owner or beneficiary is a NM resident. 0.30% (asset-based mgmt fee)
Sales Charges	$0, but if opened though a financial advisor, subject to a 3.5% initial sales charge and additional 0.25%
Underlying Fund Expenses	Approximate range: 0.41% to 1.24%
State Tax Deduction for contribution	Yes
Minimum Investment	$250 and subsequent contributions must be $100+, $25 per month for payroll deduction deposits or auto transfer from a bank account
Maximum Contribution	$251,000

(continued)

Investment Choices

Age-Based Portfolio

100% Equity Option

100% Bond Option

100% S-T Yield Option

5 blended portfolios

Funds within the Plan's
Investment Options

MFS Value A Fund

SSGA Growth and Income Fund

Janus Adviser Growth & Inc Fund

Invesco Small Co. Growth Fund

SSGA Internatl Growth Opportunities Fund

Janus Adviser Internation Fund

SSGA High Yield Bond Fund

SSGA Bond Market Fund

SSGA Yield Plus Fund

Open to Non-Residents

Yes

Can name self as beneficiary

N/A

Date existing Plan Manager
contract expires

N/A

NEW YORK

New York's College Savings Program

Plan Manager	TIAA-CREF
How to reach them	Phone: 1-877-NYSAVES Web: www.nysaves.org
Annual Fees	0.65% (asset-based mgmt fee)
Sales Charges	$0
Underlying Fund Expenses	Included in (asset-based mgmt fee)
State Tax Deduction for contribution	Yes
Minimum Investment	$25, $15 per pay period for payroll deductions
Maximum Contribution	Accepts contributions up to $100,000 or until acct balance reaches $235,000
Investment Choices	Managed Allocation Option Aggr. Managed Allocation Opt. High Equity Option Guaranteed Option

(continued)

Funds within the Plan's   College Savings Growth Fund

Investment Options   College Savings Bond Fund

College Savings Money Mkt Fund

TIAA-CREF Inst. Equity Fund

TIAA-CREF Inst. Bond Fund

TIAA-CREF Inst. Money Mkt Fund

Open to Non-Residents   Yes

Can name self as beneficiary   Yes

Date existing Plan Manager   07/30/2003
contract expires

NORTH CAROLINA

North Carolina's National College Savings Program

Plan Manager	College Foundation, Inc.
How to reach them	Phone: 1-800-600-3453 Web: www.cfnc.org/savings
Annual Fees	0.25% (asset-based mgmt fee); 0.10% for balances in Seligman CollegeHorizonFunds
Sales Charges	$0
Underlying Fund Expenses	NCM/Legg Mason Aggr Stock Fund approx 0.65%; Wachovia Balanced Fund approx 0.58%; Dependable Income Fund 0.05%; Seligman CollegeHorizonFunds approximate range: 0.58% to 1.16%
State Tax Deduction for contribution	No
Minimum Investment	$5, but a $25 annual fee is charged for balances under $1,000 unless in auto investment plan
Maximum Contribution	$268,804

(continued)

Investment Choices   Age-Based Portfolio (Seligman CollegeHorizonsFunds)

             Aggressive Stock Fund

             Balanced Fund

             Dependable Income Fund

             Any of the 22 portfolios avail in

               Seligman CollegeHorizonsFund

Funds within the Plan's   N/A
Investment Options

Open to Non-Residents   Yes

Can name self as beneficiary N/A

Date existing Plan Manager   N/A
contract expires

(continued)

Seligman CollegeHorizonFunds – Advisor-sold

Plan Manager	College Foundation, Inc. and J&W Seligman
How to reach them	Phone: 1-800-600-3453 Web: www.seligman529.com
Annual Fees	$25 annual maintenance fee, waived for account balance more than $25,000 0.25% (asset-based mgmt fee) plus extra fees/loads for accounts opened through a financial advisor under three alternative fee schedules
Sales Charges	$0
Underlying Fund Expenses	Approximate range: 0.58% to 1.16%
State Tax Deduction for contribution	No
Minimum Investment	$250 initial, $100 subsequent ($25 fee if account balance remains below $1,000). $100 for auto investment plan through bank transfer or $25 for payroll deduct.
Maximum Contribution	$268,804
Investment Choices	Age-based Portfolio 22 portfolio opts under the age-based plan

(continued)

Funds within the Plan's Investment Options   N/A

Open to Non-Residents   Yes

Can name self as beneficiary   N/A

Date existing Plan Manager contract expires   N/A

NORTH DAKOTA
College SAVE

Plan Manager	Morgan Stanley
How to reach them	Phone: 1-866-728-3529 Web: www.collegesave4u.com
Annual Fees	$30 annual maintenance fee, waived for No. and So. Dakota residents
Sales Charges	$0
Underlying Fund Expenses	Approximate range: 0.68% to 1.22%
State Tax Deduction for contribution	No
Minimum Investment	$25, $300 acct balance by end of first year
Maximum Contribution	$168,000
Investment Choices	3 Age-Based Options Aggressive Moderate Conservative Aggr Opt (incl. actively managed equity fund) Aggr Opt (incl. index equity fund) Balanced Opt (incl. actively managed equity fund) Balanced Opt (incl index eq fund)

(continued)

Funds within the Plan's   N/A
Investment Options

Open to Non-Residents   Yes (not until mid-2002)

Can name self as beneficiary   N/A

Date existing Plan Manager   N/A
contract expires

Ohio

Putnam CollegeAdvantage Savings Plan

Plan Manager	Putnam Investments
How to reach them	Phone: 1-800-225-1581 Web: www.putnaminvestments.com
Annual Fees	$25 annual maintenance fee waived if: i) account balance is $25,000 or more; ii) if you participate in an employer-sponsored plan; or, iii) if you make deposits of $50 per month through payroll deduction or auto. bank transfers. Choose b/w A shares (3.50% to 5.75% sales load and 0.55% annual fee), B shares (0% to 5.0% deferred sales charge if acct is terminated w/in 6 yrs and 1.10% annual fee), and C shares (0.80% annual fee)
Sales Charges	$0
Underlying Fund Expenses	Approximate range: 0.49% to 1.23%
State Tax Deduction for contribution	Yes
Minimum Investment	$25, or $15 per month in an auto. contribution plan
Maximum Contribution	$232,000

(continued)

Investment Choices	Age-Based Portfolio
	Blended Fund Options
	Balanced
	Growth
	Aggressive Growth
	10 individual asset class opts
Funds within the Plan's	Investors Fund
Investment Options	Growth and Income Fund (A Fund)
	Capital Opportunities Fund (A Fund)
	International Growth Fund
	New Opportunities Fund
	Voyager Fund
	New Value Fund
	International Voyager Fund
	Income Fund
	High Yield Trust II
	Money Market Fund
Open to Non-Residents	Yes
Can name self as beneficiary	N/A
Date existing Plan Manager contract expires	N/A

(continued)

Ohio CollegeAdvantage Savings Plan

Plan Manager	Putnam Investments
How to reach them	Phone: 1-800-AFFORD-IT Web: www.collegeadvantage.com
Annual Fees	$25 annual maintenance fee waived if: i) account balances of 25,000 or more; ii) you make deposits of $50 or more through payroll deduction or auto bank transfers; none for Guaranteed Savings Option 0.99% (asset-based mgmt fee) for Putnam options (direct sold); none for Guaranty Savings Option
Sales Charges	$0
Underlying Fund Expenses	Included in asset-based mgmt fee
State Tax Deduction for contribution	Yes
Minimum Investment	$15
Maximum Contribution	$232,000

(continued)

Investment Choices

Age-Based Portfolio

10 asset class options (individual funds)

4 asset allocation options

Balanced Portfolio

Growth Portfolio

Aggressive Growth Portfolio

Guaranteed Savings Opt

Funds within the Plan's Investment Options

N/A

Open to Non-Residents

No

Can name self as beneficiary

N/A

Date existing Plan Manager contract expires

N/A

OKLAHOMA

Oklahoma College Savings Plan

Plan Manager	TIAA-CREF Tuition Financing, Inc.
How to reach them	Phone: 1-877-654-7284
	Web: www.ok4saving.org
Annual Fees	0.60% annual asset based fee
Sales Charges	$0
Underlying Fund Expenses	Approximate range: 0.18% to 0.24%
State Tax Deduction for contribution	Yes
Minimum Investment deposits	$25 initial, $15 per pay period for payroll deduction
Maximum Contribution	$235,000
Investment Choices	Managed Allocation
	100% Equity Option
	Guaranteed Option

(continued)

Funds within the Plan's   Instutional Growth Equity Fund

Investment Options   Inst. Growth and Income Fund

Inst. International Equity Fund

Institutional Bond Fund

Institutional Money Market Fund

Open to Non-Residents   Yes

Can name self as beneficiary   N/A

Date existing Plan Manager   1/12007

contract expires

OREGON

Oregon College Savings Plan

Plan Manager	Strong Capital Mgmt, Inc.
How to reach them	Phone: 1-866-772-8464 Web:www.oregoncollegesavings.com
Annual Fees	$30 annual maintenance fee waived for: i) Oregon residents; ii) account balances greater than $25,000; or, iii) those enrolled in the automatic investment plan 1.275%—asset-based mgmt fee (additional expenses in the broker sold plan)
Sales Charges	$0 – direct sold plan
Underlying Fund Expenses	Included in (asset-based mgmt fee)
State Tax Deduction for contribution	Yes
Minimum Investment	$250 initial, $25 subsequent. $25 initial and subsequent for automatic investment or payroll deduction
Maximum Contribution	$150,000

(continued)

Investment Choices

Age-based portfolio (Years To College Option)

3 non-evolving portfolios

Aggressive Option

Moderate Option

Conservative Option

Funds within the Plan's

Investment Options

Strong Foreign MajorMarkets Fund

Strong Growth Fund

Strong Opportunity Fund

Strong Advisor U.S. Value Fund

Strong Corporate Bond Fund

Strong Govt. Securities Fund

Strong S-T Bond Fund

Strong Advantage Fund

Strong Heritage Money Fund

Open to Non-Residents

Yes

Can name self as beneficiary

N/A

Date existing Plan Manager

contract expires

N/A

PENNSYLVANIA

Plan is under development and set to launch in 2002.

RHODE ISLAND
CollegBoundFund

Plan Manager	Alliance Capital
How to reach them	Phone: 1-888-324-5057 Web: www.collegeboundfund.com
Annual Fees	$25 annual maintenance fee, waived if RI resident or account balance is more than $25,000 or you contribute through an automatic plan or payroll deduction. A fee is charged on the age-based portfolios to the extent the blended mutual fund exps are less than a min ratio (0.90% to 1.10%); non-resid and broker-sold accts must choose b/w A shares (4.25% sales load and additl 0.25% ann fee), B shares (0%-0.4% def sales chg if acct is termin. w/in 4 yrs and 1.00% addtl ann fee), and C shares (1.00% addtl ann fee)
Sales Charges	$0
Underlying Fund Expenses	Fund expense ratios range from 0.68% to 1.67%
State Tax Deduction for contribution	No
Minimum Investment	$1,000 initial and subsequent contributions must be at least $50 ($5,000 aggregate account balance needed to invest in the 9 individual mutual funds)
Maximum Contribution	$265,620

(continued)

Investment Choices

Age-Based Portfolio

Age-Based Aggressive Growth Emphasis Portfolio

Age-Based Growth Emphasis Portfolio

Aggressive Growth Equity Portfolio

Growth Equity Portfolio

Balanced Portfolio

Principal-Protection Income Portfolio

9 individual mutual funds

**Funds within the Plan's
Investment Options**

Alliance Fund

Growth and Income Fund

Premier Growth Fund

Quasar Institutional Fund

Alliance Bernstein Internat'l Value Fund

Alliance Bernstein SmallCap Value Fund

High Yield Fund

Bond Fund – U.S Govt Portfolio

Bond Fund – Quality Bond Portfolio

AFD Exchange Reserves

Technology Fund, Inc.

Open to Non-Residents

Yes

Can name self as beneficiary

N/A

**Date existing Plan Manager
contract expires**

06/30/2005

SOUTH CAROLINA

Future Scholar 529 College Savings Plan

Plan Manager	Bank of America Advisors, LLC
How to reach them	Phone: 1-888-244-5674
	Web: www.futurescholar.com
Annual Fees	0.20% (asset-based fee), $25 annual maintenance fee (waived for SC residents and employees of Bank of America)
Sales Charges	Initial $25 maintenance fee, waived for SC residents and employees of Bank of America
Underlying Fund Expenses	Approximate range: 0.20% to 1.23%
State Tax Deduction for contribution	Yes
Minimum Investment	Direct sold plan: $250 initial, and $50 subsequent. No minimum for payroll deduction accounts
Maximum Contribution	$250,000

(continued)

Investment Choices	Aggressive Growth Portfolio
	Growth Portfolio
	Balanced Growth Portfolio
	Balanced Portfolio
	Income and Gr. Portfolio
	Income Portfolio
	Automatic Allocation Portfolio
	Single Fund Portfolios
	LargeCap Index
	MidCap Index
	Stable Capital
Funds within the Plan's	Nations LargeCap Index Fund
Investment Options	Nations MidCap Index Fund
	Nations SmallCap Index Fund
	Nations International Value Fund
	Nations Bond Fund
	Nations Short-Term Income Fund
	Nations Cash Reserves
Open to Non-Residents	Yes
Can name self as beneficiary	Yes
Date existing Plan Manager contract expires	01/01/2012

SOUTH DAKOTA

CollegeAccess 529

Plan Manager	PIMCO Funds
How to reach them	Phone: 1-866-529-7462 Web: www.collegeaccess529.com
Annual Fees	$0 annual fee (direct accts) $0 asset-based mgmt fee (direct accts)
Sales Charges	$0 (direct accts)
Underlying Fund Expenses	0.35% to 1.41% asset-based mgmt fee (direct accts)
State Tax Deduction for contribution	N/A, no state income tax
Minimum Investment	$250 initial, or $50 per mos through auto investment plan
Maximum Contribution	$305,000
Investment Choices	Age Based Option Real Return Plus Portfolio (direct accts)
Funds within the Plan's Investment Options	N/A
Open to Non-Residents	Yes
Can name self as beneficiary	N/A
Date existing Plan Manager contract expires	N/A

TENNESSEE

Tennessee's BEST Savings Plan

Plan Manager	TIAA-CREF
How to reach them	Phone: 1-888-486-BEST Web: www.tnbest.com
Annual Fees	0.95% (asset-based mgmt fee)
Sales Charges	$0
Underlying Fund Expenses	Included in asset based fee
State Tax Deduction for contribution	No
Minimum Investment	$25, $15 per pay period for payroll deduction deposits
Maximum Contribution	$235,000
Investment Choices	Age Based Portfolio
Funds within the Plan's Investment Options	N/A
Open to Non-Residents	Yes
Can name self as beneficiary	N/A
Date existing Plan Manager contract expires	N/A

TEXAS

Plan is under development.

UTAH

Utah Educational Savings Plan Trust

Plan Manager State agency

How to reach them Phone: 800-418-2551
Web: www.uesp.org

Annual Fees $0 for fixed income option, otherwise $5 per $1000 up to $25 annual maintenance fee. $0 for fixed income option, otherwise 0.25% (asset-based mgmt fee).

Sales Charges $0

Underlying Fund Expenses Approx. range: 0% to 0.7%

State Tax Deduction for contribution Yes

Minimum Investment $25, and scheduled savings of at least $300 per year.

Maximum Contribution $101,650, but participants can save more for a beneficiary who plans to attend a more expensive college. A participant can designate a non-Utah college and save up to $175,000.

(continued)

Investment Choices

Money Market/Endowment

Stocks/Bonds/Money Market

Stocks/Bonds

Stocks

Funds within the Plan's
Investment Options

Public Treasurer's Invest. Fund

Vanguard Institutional Index Fund

Vanguard Total Bond Mkt Index Fund

Open to Non-Residents

Yes

Can name self as beneficiary

N/A

Date existing Plan Manager
contract expires

N/A

VERMONT

Vermont Higher Education Investment Plan

Plan Manager	TIAA-CREF
How to reach them	Phone: 1-800-637-5860 Web: www.vsac.org
Annual Fees	0.80% for the TIAA-CREF portfolios only (none for the Income Interest Option)
Sales Charges	$0
Underlying Fund Expenses	Included in asset-based mgmt fee
State Tax Deduction for contribution	No
Minimum Investment	$25, $15 per pay period for payroll deduction deposits
Maximum Contribution	$240,100
Investment Choices	Managed Allocation Option 100% Equity Option Interest Income Option
Funds within the Plan's Investment Options	N/A
Open to Non-Residents	Yes
Can name self as beneficiary	N/A
Date existing Plan Manager contract expires	N/A

VIRGINIA

CollegeAmerica

Plan Manager	Virginia College Savings Plan and American Funds
How to reach them	Phone: 1-800-421-4120 Web: www.americanfunds.com/ CollegeAmerica529SavingsPlan.html
Annual Fees	$10 annual maintenance fee. Each share class has different asset based fees and some w/load fees
Sales Charges	$10 enrollment fee
Underlying Fund Expenses	Varying expense ratios
State Tax Deduction for contribution	Yes
Minimum Investment	$250 per fund initially ($1,000 for Cash Mgmt Trust of America), subsequent are $50 per fund.
Maximum Contribution	$250,000
Investment Choices	21 individual mutual funds

(continued)

Funds within the Plan's
Investment Options

AMCAP Fund

EuroPacific Growth Fund

The Growth Fund of America

The New Economy Fund

New Perspective Fund

New World Fund

SMALLCAP World Fund

American Mutual Fund

Capital World Gr. & Income Fund

Fundamental Investors

The Investment Co. of America

Washington Mutual Investors Fund

Capital Income Builder

The Income Fund of America

American Balanced Fund

American High-Income Trust

The Bond Fund of America

Capital World Bond Fund

Intermediate Bond Fund of Am.

U.S Govt Securities Fund

The Cash Mgmt Trust of Am.

Open to Non-Residents   Yes

Can name self as beneficiary   Yes

Date existing Plan Manager   N/A
contract expires

(continued)

Virginia Education Savings Trust (VEST)

Plan Manager	State agency (VA College Savings Plan)
How to reach them	Phone: 1-888-567-0540
	Web: www.virginia529.com
Annual Fees	0
Sales Charges	$85 enrollment fee
Underlying Fund Expenses	Approximate range: 0.85% to 1.00% (includes all program operating expenses)
State Tax Deduction for contribution	Yes
Minimum Investment	$25 and $250 minimum in first 12 months
Maximum Contribution	$250,000
Investment Choices	8 age-based portfolios
	4 non-evolving portfolios
	Vanguard LifeStrategy Growth Fund (aggressive)
	Vanguard LifeStrategy Moderate Growth Fund (moderate)
	Vanguard LifeStrategy Income Fund (conservative)
	Vanguard Prime Money Market Fund (money market)

(continued)

Funds within the Plan's
Investment Options

Vanguard 500 Index Fund

Rothschild Asset Mgmt, Inc. (small/mid-cap
     domestic equity fund)

Vanguard Small Cap Index Fund

The American Funds' EuroPacific Growth Fund

Templeton Foreign Equity Series

Western Asset Mgmt (Fixed Inc Fund)

PRIMCO Stable Value Fund

Open to Non-Residents   Yes

Can name self as beneficiary   Yes

Date existing Plan Manager   N/A
contract expires

WASHINGTON

Plan is under development.

WASHINGTON, D.C.

Plan is under development.

WEST VIRGINIA

SMART 529 – College Savings Option

Plan Manager	Hartford Life
How to reach them	Phone: 866-574-3542 Web: www.smart529.com
Annual Fees	$25 annual maintenance fee is waived for: i) WV residents; ii) account balances of $25,000 or more; and, iii) accounts enrolled in automatic contributions 1.16% of assets in direct-sold plan (ann. asset-based mgmt fees).
Sales Charges	$0
Underlying Fund Expenses	N/A
State Tax Deduction for contribution	Yes
Minimum Investment	Direct-sold plan: $100 initial lump sum and $15 subsequent, or $15 per month.
Maximum Contribution	$265,620
Investment Choices	Age-based portfolio Aggressive Growth Growth Balanced

(continued)

Funds within the Plan's   Hartford Capital Apprec. Fund

Investment Options   Hartford Mid-Cap Fund

Hartford Global Leaders Fund

Hartford Stock Fund

Hartford Dividend & Growth Fund

Hart. Bond Income Strategy Fund

Hartford Money Mkt Fund

Open to Non-Residents   Yes

Can name self as beneficiary   Yes

Date existing Plan Manager   02/2012
contract expires

WISCONSIN

EdVest College Savings Program

Plan Manager	Strong Investments
How to reach them	Phone: 1-888-EDVEST-WI Web: www.edvestonline.com
Annual Fees	$10, waived w/automatic deposits or acct balances over $25,000. 1.25%, more if opened through a broker (asset-based mgmt fee)
Sales Charges	$20 enrollment fee
Underlying Fund Expenses	Included in asset-based mgmt fee
State Tax Deduction for contribution	Yes
Minimum Investment	$250, or $25 per month
Maximum Contribution	$246,000
Investment Choices	Age-Based Portfolio Index Portfolio Aggressive Portfolio Moderate Portfolio Balanced Portfolio Bond Portfolio 3 Tuition Unit Options (Plan A, Plan B, or Plan C)

(continued)

Funds within the Plan's
Investment Options

Strong International Stock Fund

Strong Growth Fund

Strong Index 500 Fund

Strong Opportunity Fund

Strong Advisor U.S. Value Fund

Strong Advisor Bond Fund

Strong Govt Securities Fund

Strong Short-Term Bond Fund

Strong Advantage Fund

Open to Non-Residents   Yes

Can name self as beneficiary   N/A

Date existing Plan Manager   N/A
contract expires

(continued)

Tomorrow's Scholar College Savings Plan

Plan Manager   Strong Investments

How to reach them   Phone: 1-866-677-6933
                                     Web: www.tomorrowsscholar.com

Annual Fees $10, waived w/automatic deposits or acct
                                     balances over $25,000.

                                     1.27% (asset-based mgmt fee)—additional fees
                                     paid to financial advisor

Sales Charges $20 enrollment fee

Underlying Fund Expenses   Included in (asset-based mgmt fee)

State Tax Deduction   Yes
for contribution

Minimum Investment $250, or waived if a $25 monthly automatic
                                     investment plan option is selected

Maximum Contribution $246,000

Investment Choices   Fixed Allocation Options Aggr. Portfolio
                                     Balanced Portfolio
                                     Conservative Portfolio
                                     Years-to-Enrollment Options
                                     Aggr. Portfolio
                                     Balanced Portfolio
                                     Conservative Portfolio

(continued)

Funds within the Plan's Investment Options	AXP International Fund
	AXP New Dimensions Fund
	AXP Equity Select Fund
	AXP Diversified Equity Income Fund
	Strong Growth Fund
	Strong Opportunity Fund
	Strong Advisor U.S Value Fund
	AXP Bond Fund
	AXP Federal Income Fund
	Strong Corporate Bond Fund
	Strong Govt Securities Fund
	Strong Short-Term Bond Fund
	AXP Cash Management Fund
	Strong Advantage Fund
Open to Non-Residents	Yes
Can name self as beneficiary	N/A
Date existing Plan Manager contract expires	N/A

WYOMING

The College Achievement Plan

Plan Manager	Mercury Advisors
How to reach them	Phone: 1-877-529-2655 Web: www.collegeachievementplan.com
Annual Fees	$25, waived for WY residents or balances of $25,000+ 0.95% (asset-based mgmt fee)
Sales Charges	$0
Underlying Fund Expenses	0.85% to 1.45%
State Tax Deduction for contribution	No. Wyoming has no state inc. tax
Minimum Investment	$1,000 ($250 for WY residents), subsequent must be at least $50
Maximum Contribution	$245,000
Investment Choices	Age-Adjusted Portfolio 100% Equity Portfolio 75% Equity Portfolio Balanced Portfolio Fixed Income Portfolio
Funds within the Plan's Investment Options	N/A
Open to Non-Residents	Yes
Can name self as beneficiary	Yes
Date existing Plan Manager contract expires	05/03/2009

APPENDIX C

STATE PROGRAM
INTERNET LINKS

The following are the world wide web addresses for the various College Savings Plans now available. You will see that some states have entered into agreements with more than one Plan Manager, so in these cases there is more than one plan available. Some states have not implemented their College Savings Plan as of the date of publication, and in those cases, no web address is listed.

Alaska	U Alaska http://www.uacollegesavings.com
Alaska	Manulife http://www.manulifecollegesavings.com
Alaska	T. Rowe Price http://www.troweprice.com/collegesavings
Arizona	College Savings Bank http://arizona.collegesavings.com
Arizona	Waddell & Reed InvestEd http://www.waddell.com

Arizona	Securities Mgmt & Research, Inc. http://www.smrinvest.com/College
Arkansas	Gift College http://www.thegiftplan.com
California	Golden State ScholarShare http://www.scholarshare.com
Colorado	CollegeInvest/Scholars Choice http://www.scholars-choice.com
Connecticut	CHET http://www.aboutchet.com
Delaware	Delaware College Inv. Plan http://www.fidelity.com/delaware
Idaho	Ideal http://www.idsaves.org
Illinois	Bright Start http://www.brightstartsavings.com
Indiana	CollegeChoice http://www.collegechoiceplan.com
Iowa	College Savings Iowa http://www.collegesavingsiowa.com
Kansas	Learning Quest http://www.learningquestsavings.com
Kentucky	Kentucky Education Savings Plan Trust http://www.kentuckytrust.org

Louisiana	START	http://www.osfa.state.la.us/START.htm
Maine	NextGen	http://www.nextgenplan.com
Maryland	College Savings Plan of Maryland	http://www.collegesavingsmd.org
Massachusetts	U.Fund	http://www.mefa.org
Michigan	Michigan Education Savings Plan	http://www.misaves.com
Minnesota	Minnesota College Savings Plan	http://www.mnsaves.org
Mississippi	Mississippi Affordable College Savings Plan	http://www.collegesavingsms.com
Missouri	MO$T	http://www.missourimost.org
Montana	Montana Family Education Savings Program	http://montana.collegesavings.com
Nebraska	College Savings Plan of Nebraska	http://www.planforcollegenow.com
Nebraska	AIM	http://www.aimfunds.com

Nebraska	TD Waterhouse http://www.tdwaterhouse.com **NOTE:** *This is a new plan with no information other than this website.*
Nevada	American Skandia http://www.americanskandia.com
Nevada	America's College Savings Plan http://www.americas529plan.com
New Hampshire	Advisor College Investing Plan http://www.advisorxpress.com
New Hampshire	Unique College Investing Plan http://www.fidelity.com/unique
New Jersey	New Jersey Better Educational Savings Trust http://www.hesaa.org/students/njbest
New Mexico	The Education's Plan's College Saving Program http://www.theeducationplan.com
New Mexico	Scholar's Edge http://www.scholarsedge529.com **NOTE:** *This is a new plan with no information other than this website.*
New Mexico	CollegeSense http://www.collegesense.com
New York	New York's College Savings Program http://www.nysaves.com

North Carolina	National College Savings Program http://http://www.cfnc.org/savings
North Carolina	Seligman College HorizonFunds http://www.seligman529.com
North Dakota	College SAVE http://www.collegesave4u.com
Ohio	CollegeAdvantage Savings Plan http://www.collegeadvantage.com
Ohio	Putnam CollegeAdvantage Savings Plan http://www.putnaminvestments.com
Oklahoma	Oklahoma College Savings Plan http://www.ok4saving.org
Oregon	Oregon College Savings Plan http://www.oregoncollegesavings.com
Rhode Island	CollegeBoundFund http://www.collegeboundfund.com
South Carolina	Future Scholar http://www.futurescholar.com
Tennessee	Tennessee's BEST http://www.tnbest.com
Utah	Utah's Educational Savings Plan Trust http://www.uesp.org
Vermont	Vermont Higher Education Investment Plan http://www.vsac.org

Virginia	CollegeAmerica http://www.americanfunds.com/ CollegeAmerica529SavingsPlan.html
Virginia	VEST http://www.virginia529.com
West Virginia	SMART 529 http://www.smart529.com
Wisconsin	EdVest http://www.edvest.com
Wisconsin	Tomorrow's Scholar http://www.tomorrowsscholar.com
Wyoming	The College Achievement Plan http://www.collegeachievementplan.com

INDEX

401(k), 4, 18, 24, 29, 35, 87

A

account owner, 4, 6, 7, 9, 10, 29, 45, 46, 47, 53–56, 69
  contingent owner, 71
  successor owner, 54, 69
adjusted gross income, 23, 25
advisor, 5, 57–62, 78, 87
advisor plans, 57, 87
Affinity, 94
age-based investment options, 7
age-based portfolio, 58
alcohol, 20
annual account statement, 10
annuities, 18
appreciation, 2, 5, 6, 66
asset-based management fees, 5
assets, 2, 4, 5, 6, 9, 10, 11, 15, 18, 19, 20, 21, 22, 24, 25, 27, 28, 29, 33, 46, 54, 57, 67, 71, 83
associates degree, 15, 34
automobile, 34

B

BabyMint™, 93–94
bachelors degree, 15, 34
beneficiary, 4, 6, 7, 9–10, 11, 23, 25, 27, 29, 45–52, 53–56, 66, 67, 69, 71, 83, 94
  change, 7, 29, 46–49
  designated, 83

Beneficiary Change Form, 47
benefits, 75–82
bonds, 19, 23, 24
books, 10, 34, 68
broker, 5

C

capital, 6, 58
cash, 4, 6
certificates of deposits, 19, 23, 24
charity, 83–92
chase the best return, 7
child not yet born, 46
collateral, 4, 9
college credits, 15
commission, 87
community college, 15
Congress, 1, 3, 7, 9, 12, 35, 59, 72
consumer, 2, 6, 7, 9, 94
contribution limit, 25, 49
corporate-sponsored plans, 60, 87–90
corporation, 60, 76, 93
Coverdell Savings Account, 11, 18, 22–25
Crummey trust. *See trusts*
custodial accounts, 19–22, 46
custodian, 19, 20

D

death, 22, 25, 51, 53–54, 63, 69, 70–71
debts, 9
deduction, 20
defined benefit plans, 18
disqualifying distribution, 9
"double dip" opportunity, 68
drug abuse, 20

E

Economic Growth and Tax Relief
    Reconciliation Act of 2001
    (EGTRRA), 10, 34
Education IRA. *See Coverdell Savings
    Account*
eligible educational institution, 5,
    11–13, 34
employee, 75–82
employee benefit, 75–82
employer-sponsored plans, 75–82
employers, 75–82
enrollment fees, 5
estate planning, 9, 15, 21, 27, 53,
    63–74
estate tax. *See taxes*

F

family member. *See member of the
    family*
federal student aid program, 11, 34
fiduciary shield, 60
financial aid, 20, 51, 53
financial service firm, 3, 26
front-end loading, 64

G

gains, 5, 6, 22, 28, 34, 35, 67
generation-skipping transfer tax. *See
    taxes*
gift tax. *See taxes*
gifts, 21, 27, 63, 69, 72
graduate school, 11, 15
grandchildren, 8, 29, 55, 67
grandparents, 8, 27, 51, 53, 68

H

Higher Education Act of 1965, 34
HOPE Scholarships, 11, 29

I

income, 6, 7, 9, 10, 19, 20, 21, 23, 25,
    28, 70
institutional approach, 3
insurance, 18, 75, 76, 94
    dental, 75
    life, 75
    long term care, 76
    medical, 75
interest, 28
Internal Revenue Code (IRC), 1, 33,
    45, 83
    Section 501, 83
    Section 529, 1–3, 33, 45, 59
Internal Revenue Service (IRS), 2, 84
investment, 2, 3, 4, 5, 6–8, 17, 19, 21,
    24, 26, 28, 34, 35, 50, 57, 58, 77, 78
    firms, 3
    options, 5
IRA, 4, 35
irrevocable trust. *See trusts*

J

joint account, 20

K

kiddie tax, 6, 19, 21, 28

L

law school, 34
lawsuit, 20, 60
legal capacity, 19
Lifetime Learning Credits, 11, 29
liquidation, 6
loan, 9

M

maintenance fee, 5
matching contributions, 87–88
medical school, 34
member of the family, 47–49, 50, 53, 67, 69
money, 1, 2, 8, 9, 10, 19, 28, 35, 78, 87
mutual funds, 19, 23, 24, 58

N

non-residents, 5

O

options, 19
owner. *See account owner*

P

parents, 1, 6, 8, 19, 20, 22, 27, 28, 48, 51
participating educational institution, 1
payroll deduction, 75
penalty, 27, 45, 47, 50. *See taxes*
pension plans, 18, 35
phases out, 25
Plan Manager, 3, 5, 7, 8, 9, 47, 49, 50, 54, 57, 58, 60, 77, 83, 87, 94
portfolio, 17, 58
post secondary trade, 11
post-secondary education, 15, 34
pre-paid tuition plan, 1, 25–27
probate, 54
professional advisor. *See advisor*
professional degree, 15, 34
profit sharing plans, 18, 35
property, 70

Q

QTIP trust. *See Qualified Terminable Interest Property Trust (QTIP)*
qualified employee, 86
qualified higher education expenses, 2, 4, 8, 10–13, 22, 33, 34–43, 69, 83
Qualified Terminable Interest Property Trust (QTIP), 70

R

re-filling of the account, 84, 89
real estate, 19, 24
reimbursement, 87
residents, 5
retail plans, 57
retirement, 18, 24, 29, 35, 75, 88
returns, 5, 26
risk tolerance, 4, 5
risk-adjusted options, 7
room and board, 8, 10, 34, 68

S

savings, 1, 6
scholarships, 8, 20, 83–92
Section 2503(b) trust. *See trusts*
Section 2503(c) trust. *See trusts*
Section 529. *See Internal Revenue Code (IRC)*
securities, 4, 6
special needs children, 10, 11, 34
spouse, 45, 48
static portfolios, 7
stocks, 4, 6, 19, 23, 24
student, 10
student aid program. *See federal student aid program*
successor owner. *See account owner*
sunset, 11, 12, 40
supplies, 10, 34, 68
surrogate law, 54

T

tax-deferred, 17, 18, 21, 22, 24, 26, 28, 29, 46, 65, 67, 83
tax-favored savings, 10, 34
taxes, 1, 6, 10, 12, 15, 17–32, 33–44, 47, 53, 57, 63, 68, 77, 79, 84, 94
  benefits, 2, 4, 12, 15
  bracket, 28, 39, 87
  credit, 29
  deduction, 5, 35–39, 50, 57
  estate, 9, 21, 22, 25, 63, 68, 71
  evasion, 84
  federal, 4, 20, 28, 35, 63, 71, 77, 84
  generation-skipping transfer tax, 9, 69
  gift, 9, 22, 25, 53, 63, 68, 69
  income, 9, 12, 17, 19, 23, 27, 28, 35, 49, 50, 67, 79
  penalty, 9, 10, 12, 33, 49, 67
  state, 28, 36, 50, 57, 79
trustee, 71
trusts, 27, 53, 55, 70–74
  by-pass, 70
  Crummey, 28
  irrevocable, 27
  Section 2503(b), 28
  Section 2503(c), 27
tuition, 1, 8, 10, 25, 26–27, 34, 68
tuition credits, 1, 25, 27, 29

U

UGMA/UTMA. *See Uniform Gift to Minors Act (UGMA), or Uniform Transfers to Minors Act (UTMA)*
undergraduate, 8
Uniform Gift to Minors Act (UGMA), 6, 19, 46
Uniform Transfers to Minors Act (UTMA), 6, 19, 46
Upromise™, 93–94

V

vocational school, 11, 15, 34

W

will, 54, 70
withdrawal, 5, 9, 22, 28, 39–44

ABOUT THE AUTHORS

Richard A. Feigenbaum is an attorney in a private law practice in Wellesley, Massachusetts. His practice is primarily comprised of estate planning and estate administration (probate law), specifically focusing on the use of trusts, charitable gifts, and other tax saving and probate avoidance devices. Mr. Feigenbaum received his Law Degree, as well as a Graduate Law Degree in Taxation, from Boston University School of Law. He has authored a book on Probate Law, published by Sphinx/Sourcebooks and has taught Probate Law for the Northeastern University Financial Planning Institute and the Professional Paralegal Program. Mr. Feigenbaum has co-authored "Estate Administration for the Paralegal," published by Massachusetts Continuing Legal Education, Inc. He is a member of the Boston Estate Planning Council, is listed in "Who's Who in Executives and Professionals," and is a frequent lecturer on estate planning topics for charities and financial services organizations.

David J. Morton is a Managing Director of Wachovia Securities in Boston, Massachusetts, and is involved in the management of assets for individuals and corporations and in capital raising activities for businesses. He is a Registered Investment Advisor and is the co-recipient of the 2001 New England Benefits Council Award for his work in bringing the College Savings 529 Plan to industry. Mr. Morton is a graduate cum laude from Bowdoin College and resides with his family in Dover, Massachusetts.